SERMONS ON THE PRAYER OF JABEZ

Compiled by
Stanley Barnes

AMBASSADOR

BELFAST, NORTHERN IRELAND
GREENVILLE, USA

Sermons on the Prayer of Jabez
© Copyright 2002 Stanley Barnes

ISBN 1 84030 125 2

Ambassador Publications
a division of
Ambassador Productions Ltd.
Providence House
Ardenlee Street,
Belfast,
BT6 8QJ
Northern Ireland
www.ambassador-productions.com

Emerald House
427 Wade Hampton Blvd.
Greenville
SC 29609, USA
www.emeraldhouse.com

SERMONS ON THE PRAYER OF JABEZ

AMBASSADOR

BELFAST, NORTHERN IRELAND
GREENVILLE, USA

SERMONS ON
THE PRAYER OF JABEZ

"And Jabez called on the god of Israel, saying, O that Thou wouldest bless me indeed, and enlarge my coast, and that Thine hand might be with me, and that Thou wouldest keep me from evil, that it may not grieve me! And God granted him that which he requested."

INTRODUCTION

The dawn of a new millennium has witnessed an amazing renewal of interest in the Prayer of Jabez, found in I Chronicles 4 vs.9-10. The Scriptures record no fewer than 650 definite prayers of which no less that 450 have recorded answers.

The Apostle James reminds us that 'the effectual fervent prayer of a righteous man availeth much.'

God answered the prayers of men and women of the Bible such as Abraham, Moses, David, Hannah, Deborah and Mary, and even yet He still delights in answering the effectual fervent prayers of righteous men.

The prayer of Jabez is a classic illustration in Scripture of answered prayer, and my desire would be that this collection of sermons will inspire each one of us to enrol in the school of prayer, asking as the disciples did, 'Lord teach us to pray.'

Stanley Barnes
November 2002

CONTENTS

CLARENCE EDWARD NOBLE MᶜCARTNEY

C larence Edward Noble McCartney was born in 1879 in Northwood, Ohio. He graduated from the university of Wisconsin, Princeton University and Princeton Theological Seminary. He was ordained to the ministry of the Presbyterian Church and his first pastorate was in First Church, Paterson, New Jersey. He then went on to serve in Arch Street Church, Philadelphia.

In 1924 he was elected as moderator of the General Assembly of the Northern Presbyterian Church, USA and for twenty-seven years he pastured the influential First Presbyterian Church of Pittsburgh, Pennsylvania.

He was especially gifted in preaching Bible characters, and in this respect he has been called 'the American Alexander White.' He felt that there was a great advantage in such preaching in that you summoned these men themselves into the pulpit and allowed them to preach for you. They teach how God deals with our imperfections and limitations, and we learn that while He never condones our sins, the peculiar weaknesses in a disciple are not so much a fault to condemn as an infirmity to supplement.'

He was the author of more than forty publications, which included historical studies, sermons and biblical exegesis, among them *You Can Conquer Prayer at the Golden Altar, The Greatest Questions of the Bible* and *Life and Bible Epitaphs* from which this sermon was taken.

Chapter One

GOD'S SOCIAL REGISTER

"Jabez was more honourable than his brethren"
1 Chronicles 4: 9

Tables of genealogy make dull reading. When we come to them in the Bible we generally skip them and go on to something more interesting. Yet they have their place in the inspired Scriptures, and it is worth while to read through these dreary catalogues of names, for here and there, just as one finds a flower growing amid the ruins of Ephesus or Antioch, you come upon the record of some noble and useful life. Here is such a record. In the list of these men who were born, begat, and died, and are dismissed by the Chronicler, you find this exquisite and fragrant flower of biography blooming amid the ruins and relics of the past. "Jabez was more honourable than his brethren." In this graveyard of the dead here is one man of whom something more is said than merely that he was born, lived and died. He receives honourable mention for the qualities of the soul.

Most cities have what they would call a Social Register; sometimes a Blue Book, or a Red Book, wherein are inscribed the names of those who move in what is called "society". But God has His own Blue Book, where are entered the names of those who have achieved beauty of character. That is the only true distinction.

Imagine, if you can, an angel of heaven asking one of the redeemed spirits about the family, the social station in this world, of another and a recently arrived redeemed spirit! How absurd, how unthinkable for there the only distinction is the distinction of the soul.

"There is One great society alone on earth: The noble living and the noble dead."

Let us look more closely at this thumbnail biography of Jabez which we find here in the midst of this table of ancient genealogy.

1. Heredity

When you come upon the record of a remarkable life like this, distinguished for qualities of the soul, you can be certain that back of this man there is a line of worthy and godly ancestry. In the case of Jabez we are able to trace this line. He came of the Kenites, and was therefore a descendant of the Rechabites, whose chief Jonadab, in order to preserve their simplicity of manners and their morals, commanded them to dwell in tents and abstain from wine and all intoxicating liquor. Ages after, Jeremiah found these people still faithful to their vow, and the promise was given them that they should not want a man to stand before God forever.

When God chose a man to do some particular ministry, not infrequently he was set apart from the ordinary customs of life by the vow of the Nazarites which include total abstinence from strong drink. This was true of Samson, and of a far greater than Samson, John the Baptist. Thus we see that Jabez came of a godly, self-denying line of people, among whom there was plain living and high thinking. Men do not gather grapes of thorns, nor figs of thistles. Whence came John Milton with his glorious vision and gift of song? And came Oliver Cromwell with his shaking down of that which was unjust and evil? Whence, but from the Puritans, the Rechabites of that age?

The only heredity about which one is justified in boasting is the heredity of a godly ancestry. In the beautiful lines, "On the Receipt of My Mother's Picture," William Cowper says:

"My boast is not, that I deduce my birth
From loins enthroned and rulers of the earth;
But higher far my proud pretentions rise-
The son of parents passed into the skies!"

2. Overcoming Handicaps

His mother named her child Jabez, which means "he makes sorrow." "His mother called his name Jabez, saying, Because I bare him with sorrow." We wonder what lies back of that record. Did it mean that he was a posthumous child, that his father was dead? Did it mean that this mother foresaw the long, grim struggle with poverty that awaited her and him? Or did it mean that he was an unwanted child? Whatever it was, Jabez entered upon life under some kind of a handicap. What mysteries there are in life and character! Children who come into the world with the best start, and are surrounded with every advantage, stimulated with every possible training, will amount to nothing; whereas children who are flung out, as it were, into the midst of the world, with everything against them, and with apparently no chance at all, rise to usefulness and eminence and become more honourable than their brethren.

Early in the last century, the Presbyterian minister at Darlington Pennsylvania, out on his pastoral round, was riding his horse down a country lane. As he drew up before a humble cottage, he heard the sound of a woman's voice lifted in earnest prayer. As he listened he heard this widowed mother, with her boys kneeling at her side, earnestly entreating God that he would open a door for the education of these boys, so that they might become good and useful men. The pastor dismounted and went in to speak with the widow who had prayed so earnestly, and yet with a note of sorrow in her voice. Struck with the alertness of one these boys, and touched by the woman's petitions, he took the boy with him to the old Stone Academy at Darlington, and there gave him the instruction for which his mother had prayed. That boy, so handicapped in his birth, and for whom there seemed to be no opportunity, influenced more young minds in

America in the last century than any other man, for it was William Mc Guffey, the author of the famous Eclectic Readers, which reached the extraordinary circulation of 2,000,000 copies.

The Presbyterian Church celebrates this year the centennial of the achievements in Oregon of the missionaries, Henry Harman Spalding and Marcus Whitman, two of the noblest heroes in the long roll call of Presbyterian missionaries. This Henry Harman Spalding was an exception to the general law of heredity, in that he came into the world an illegitimate and unwanted child. Even the foster mother, who took him in, cast him out when he was a lad, and the boy, a stranger to all the ordinary joys of boyhood, wished that he might die. Yet he overcame the handicaps of his birth and early life and lived to write one of the most heroic pages of the modern Acts of the Apostles of Christ.

3.   Jabez Was a Man of Prayer

The others who are mentioned here were begotten, begat others in turn, and then died. That is all that is said of them. But it is written of Jabez, who is more honourable than his brethren, that "he called on the God of Israel." Of the others nothing is said, save their birth and death. But Jabez was a man of prayer. That, evidently, was the secret of the nobility of his life, and the reason for the immortality of his fame. The Holy Spirit, who delights to linger over the name of Jabez, has preserved for us the remarkable prayer which he made.

The first thing that strikes one about that prayer is its deep earnestness and urgency of petition, " O that thou wouldst bless me indeed." Jabez held that God was the source of every blessing, and that without his favour life could not be truly blessed. He asked that God would bless him *indeed*. There are blessings that shine brightly and appear to be blessings, but are not so "indeed." On the other hand, what may seem at the time anything but a blessing-adversities, hardship, pain, sorrow-may in the end prove to be a blessing "indeed." Jabez wants a real blessing, in whatever form God chooses to send it. He wants the blessing that maketh rich and addeth no sorrow therewith. Once I listened to a remarkable farewell address given by a venerable college president to the graduating class on Commencement Day. He lod them that he hoped that they would have a degree of success in life, and in their chosen callings and professions; but that his chief desire for them, and that of the college they were leaving, was that they might be men and women of God. There was a college president who prayed for his young men and young women that they might be blessed "indeed."

Jabez asked for temporal things. "O that thou wouldst enlarge my coast." We are encouraged, and in the Lord's Prayer we have the example of Christ, to pray for temporal blessings. Some people who scoff at the idea of asking God for temporal blessings, as if that were unworthy of true belivers, know better than some of the great wrestlers with God, such as Jacob, and Jabez, who asked God to enlarge his coast, and Christ, who in our Lord's Prayer taught us to say, "Give us this day our daily bread." In that great prayer spiritual and temporal good are joined together. It is right that we should ask God to bless us in "our basket and in our store."

But that phrase, "Enlarge my coast," opens a door to higher things than even the necessary good of this world. It makes us think of the larger and more abundant life, of wider sympathies, of increasing knowledge, and of deepening faith and love. What a great many people need to lift them out of their littleness, and sometimes out of their meanness and wickedness, is the enlarged coast, to see and believe and possess the greater things, and the life which is more than meat, and the body which is more than raiment.

Jabez prayed also for divine guidance. "O that thine hand might be with me." The Bible makes beautiful use of the hand of God. What you have here is a picture of God's hand on a man's shoulder, or taking the pilgrim by the hand and leading him in the way. Jabez wants the hand of God to be with him. Whichever way he turns, and in whatever he undertakes, he will do it only after asking God's guidance and seeking God's permission. We all come to times and places when we are not sure which way to turn; and yet we seem to realize that much depends, as to are future welfare and happiness, upon the decision we make or the way in which we turn. Always, at least, before we make the decission, or take one road instead of another, we can ask that God will bless the decision. Then, no matter what comes, we can be sure that there is some good and some blessing in it for us. "In all the ways acknowledge him, and he will direct thy paths."

"Through each perplexing path of Life,
Our wondering footsteps guide,
Give us each day our daily bread,
And raiment fit provide."

The last and the greatest petition of Jabez was this: "O that thou wouldest keep me from evil, that it may not grieve me!" Jabez had the true philosophy of life. The one thing from which we ought to pray to be kept is evil. The one root sorrow, the one fountainhead of woe and suffering in life, is moral evil. Nothing grieves like that. There is no sadness like the sadness of sin, there is no night like the darkness of evil. There are men and woman all about us today who carry with them some kind of grief or sorrow or pain or trouble. It may be a thorn in the flesh; it may be a disappointment of the heart; it may be a concern for a loved one; it may be a deep anxiety for the morrow. It may be a concern about the very necessities of life; it may be the sharp wounds of unkindness or ingratitude or slander or injustice. But all these are as nothing compared with the grief and pain that come to a man through sin, through the evil that is in the world. Christ taught us to repeat the prayer of Jabez when he told us to pray, "Lead us not into temptation, but deliver us from evil." And in his own great prayer on the night on which he was betrayed, when he prayed for his disciples, and for all those who in ages to come should through them believe on his name, he said, "I pray not that thou shouldst take them out of the world, but that thou shouldst keep them from the evil."

Such, then, was the prayer of Jabez. How beautiful and fragrant still is this flower which we have found amid the dusty ruins and broken stones of a forgotten world. It is a prayer that all of us would do well to make, when everyday we begin a new life and go forth into the world. The world has changed greatly in outward form since Jabez lived and died. But man has not changed; sin has not changed. It has lost nothing of its power to grieve, to wound, and to hurt. Still, with all our vaunted knowledge, we know so little of ourselves, of the world about us, and of the tomorrow. Therefore, we can all pray that God would bless us indeed, enlarge the coasts of our life, guide us with his hand, and keep us from the evil that is in the world.

The name of Jabez is forever enrolled in the Social Register of God. He was more honourable than his brethren. Strive for that distinction! Rejoice not in the passing things of this world which entertain and please for but a moment and then are gone, but rejoice rather that your names are written in Heaven, in the Lamb's book of Life.

CHARLES HADDON SPURGEON

C harles Haddon Spurgeon is undoubtedly the most famous Baptist minister of the nineteenth century. Converted in 1850, he preached his first sermon at the age of sixteen.

When he was eighteen he was invited to become the pastor of the Baptist congregation at Waterbeach, Cambridgeshire. Two years later, he was called to the New Park Street Church in London and within a year of his ministry the church was filled to overflowing. By the time he was twenty two years of age he was London's most popular preacher, and in order to facilitate the vast crowds who flocked to hear him preach, a much larger building, the Metropolitan Tabernacle, was built in 1861. It seated six thousand, and until his death in 1892, was consistently filled.

During the construction of the Tabernacle, Spurgeon preached to crowds of ten thousand in the Surrey Gardens Music Hall, and on one occasion, at the youthful age of twenty three, he preached to twenty four thousand in the Crystal Palace.

In 1855, he began to publish his sermons every Thursday, at the price of one penny, and today they make up the fifty seven volumes of The Metropolitan Tabernacle Pulpit.

This sermon was delivered by Spurgeon at the Metropolitan Tabernacle, Newington.

Chapter Two

THE PRAYER OF JABEZ

⌘

"Oh that thou wouldest bless me indeed!"
1 Chron.iv.10.

⌘

We know very little about Jabez, except that he was more honourable than his brethren, and that he was called Jabez because his mother bare him with sorrow. It will sometimes happen that where there is the most sorrow in the antecedents, there will be the most pleasure in the sequel. As the furious storm gives place to the clear sunshine, so the night of weeping precedes the morning of joy. Sorrow the harbinger; gladness the prince it ushers in. Cowper says:-

"The path of sorrow, and that path alone,
Leads to the place where sorrow is unknown."

To a great extent we find that we must sow in tears before we can reap in joy. Many of our works for Christ have cost us tears. Difficulties and disappointments have wrung our soul with anguish. Yet those projects that have cost us more than ordinary sorrow, have often turned out to be the most honourable of our undertakings. While our grief called the offspring of our desire "Benoni," the son of my sorrow, our faith has been afterwards able to give it a name of delight,

"Benjamin," the son of my right hand. You may suspect a blessing in serving God if you are enabled to persevere under many discouragements. The ship is often long coming home, because detained on the road by excess of cargo. Expect her freight to be the better when she reaches the port. More honourable than his brethren was the child whom his mother bore with sorrow. As for this Jabez, whose aim was so well pointed, his fame so far sounded, his name so lastingly embalmed-he was a man of prayer. The honour he enjoyed would not have been worth having if it had not been vigorously contested and equitably won. His devotion was the key to his promotion. Those are the best honours that come from God, the award of grace with the acknowledgement of service. When Jacob was surnamed Israel, he received his princedom after a memorable night of prayer. Surely it was far more honourable to him than if it had been bestowed upon him as a flattering distinction by some earthly emperor. The best honour is that which a man gains in communion with the Most High. Jabez, we are told, was more honourable than his brethren, and his prayer is forthwith recorded, as if to intimate that he was also more prayerful than his brethren. We are told of what petitions his prayer consisted. All through it was very significant and instructive. We have only time to take one clause of it-indeed, that one clause may be said to comprehend all the rest: "Oh that thou wouldest bless me indeed!" I commend it as a prayer for yourselves, dear brethren and sisters; one which will be available at all seasons; a prayer to begin Christian life with, a prayer to end it with, a prayer which would never be unseasonable in your joys or in your sorrows.

Oh that thou, the God of Israel, the covenant God, would bless me indeed! The very pith of the prayer seems to lie in that word "indeed." There are many varieties of blessing. Some are blessings only in name: they gratify our wishes for a moment, but permanently disappoint our expectations. They charm the eye, but pall on the taste. Others are mere temporary blessings: they perish with the using. Though for a while they regale the senses, they cannot satisfy the higher cravings of the soul. But, "Oh that thou wouldest bless me indeed!" I wot whom God blesseth shall be blessed. The thing good in itself is bestowed with the good- will of the giver, and shall be productive of so much good fortune to the recipient that it may well be esteemed as a blessing "indeed," for there is nothing comparable to it. Let the grace of God prompt it, let the choice of God appoint it, let the bounty of God confer it, and then the endowment shall be something godlike indeed; something worthy of the lips that pronounce the benediction and verily to be craved by everyone who seeks honour that is substantial and enduring. "Oh that thou wouldest bless me indeed!" Think it over, and you will see there is a depth of meaning in the expression.

We may set this in contrast with human blessings: "Oh that thou wouldest bless me indeed!" It is very delightful to be blessed by our parents, and those venerable friends whose benedictions come from their hearts, and are backed up by their prayers. Many a poor man has had no other legacy to leave his children except his blessing, but the blessing of an honest, holy, Christian father is a rich treasure to his son. One might well feel it were a thing to be deplored through life if he had lost a parent's blessing. We like to have it. The blessing of our spiritual parents is consolatory. Though we believe in no priestcraft, we like to live in the affections of those who were the means of bringing us to Christ, and from whose lips we are instructed in the things of God. And how very precious is the blessing of the poor! I do not wonder that Job treasured that up as a sweet thing. "When the ear heard me, then it blessed me." If you have relieved the widow and the fatherless, and their thanks are returned to you in benediction, it is no mean reward. But, dear friends, after all-all that parents, relatives, saints, and grateful persons can do in the way of blessing, falls very far short of what we desire to have. O Lord, we would have the blessings of our fellow-creatures, the blessings that come from their hearts; but, "Oh that *Thou* wouldest bless me indeed!" for thou canst bless with authority. Their blessings may be but words, but thine are effectual. They may often wish what they cannot do, and desire to give what they have not at their own desposal, but thy will is omnipotent. Thou dids't create the world with but a word. O that such omnipotence would now bespeak me thy blessing! Other blessings may bring us some tiny cheer, but in thy favour is life. Other blessings are mere tittles in comparison with thy blessing; for thy blessing is the title "to an inheritance incorruptible" and unfading, to "a kingdom which cannot be moved." Well therefore might David pray in another place, "With thy blessing let the house of thy servant be blessed forever." Perhaps in this place, Jabez may have put the blessing of God in contrast with the blessings of men. Men will bless thee when thou doest well for thyself. They will praise the man who is successful in business. Nothing succeeds like success. Nothing has so much the approval of the general public as a man's prosperity. Alas! They do not weigh mans actions in the balances of the sanctuary, but in quite other scales.

You will find those about you who will commend you if you are prosperous; or like Job's comforters, condemn you if you suffer adversity. Perhaps there may be some feature about their blessings that may please you, because you feel you deserve them. They commend you for your patriotism: you have been a patriot. They commend you for your generosity: you know you have been self-sacrificing. Well, but after all, what is there in the verdict of man? At a trial, the verdict of the policeman who stands in the court, or of the spectators who sit in the court-house, amounts to just nothing. The man who is being tried feels that the only thing that is of importance at all will be the verdict of the jury, and the sentence of the judge. So it will little avail us whatever we may do, how others commend or censure. Their blessings are not of any great value. But, "Oh that thou wouldest bless me," that thou wouldest say, "Well done, good and faithful servant." Commend thou the feeble service that through thy grace my heart has rendered. That will be to bless me indeed.

Men are sometimes blessed in a very fulsome sense by flattery. There are always those who, like the fox in the fable, hope to gain the cheese by praising the crow. They never saw much plumage, and no voice could be so sweet as yours. The whole of their mind is set, not on you, but what they are to gain by you. The race of flatterers is never extinct, though the flattered usually flatter themselves it is so. They may conceive that men flatter others, but all is so palpable and transparent when heaped upon themselves, that they accept it with a great deal of self-complacency, as being perhaps a little exaggerated, but after all exceeding near the truth. We are not very apt to take a large discount off the praises that others offer us; yet, were we wise, we should press to our bosom those who censure us, and we should always keep at arms length those who praise us, for those who censure us to our face cannot possibly be making a market of us; but with regard to those who extol us, rising early, and using loud sentences of praise, we may suspect, and we shall very seldom be unjust in the suspicion, that there is some other motive in the praise which they render to us than that which appears on the surface. Young man, art thou placed in a position where God honours thee? Beware of flatterers. Or hast thou come into a large estate? Hast thou abundance? There are always flies where there is honey. Beware of flattery. Young woman, art thou fair to look upon? There will be those about you that have their designs, perhaps their evil designs, in lauding thy beauty. Beware of flatterers. Turn thou aside from all these that have honey on their tongue, because of the poison of asps that is under it. Bethink thee of Solomon's caution, "meddle not with him that flattereth with his lips." Cry to God, "Deliver thou me from all this vain adulation, which nauseates my soul." So shalt thou pray to him the more fervently, "O that thou wouldest bless me indeed!" Let me have thy benediction, which never says more than it means; which never gives less than it promises. If you take then the prayer of Jabez as being put in contrast to the benedictions which come from men, you see much force in it.

But we may put in another light, and compare the blessing Jabez craved with those blessings that are temporal and transient. There are many bounties given to us mercifully by God for which we are bound to be very grateful; but we must not set too much store by them. We may accept them with gratitude, but we must not make them our idols. When we have them we have great need to cry, "Oh that thou wouldest bless me indeed, and make these inferior blessings real blessings;" and if we have them not, we should with greater vehemence cry, "Oh that we may be rich in faith, and if not blessed with these external favours, may we be blessed spiritually, and then we should be blessed indeed."

Let us review some of these mercies, and just say a word or two about them.

One of the first cravings of men's hearts is wealth. So universal the desire to gain it, that we might also say it is a natural instinct.

How many have thought if they once possessed it they should be blessed indeed! But there are ten thousand proofs that happiness consists not in the abundance which a man possesseth. So many instances are well known to you all, that I need not quote any to show that riches are not a blessing indeed. They are rather apparently than really so. Hence, it has been well said, that when we see how much a man has we envy him; but could we see how little he enjoys we should pity him. Some that have had the most easy circumstances have had the most uneasy minds. Those who have acquired all they could wish, had there wishes been at all sane, have been led by the possession of what they had to be discontented because they had not more.

> "Thus the base miser starves amidst his store,
> Broods o'er his gold, and griping still at more,
> Sits sadly pining, and believes he's poor."

Nothing is more clear to anyone who chooses to observe it, than that riches are not the chief good at whose advent sorrow flies, and in whose presence joy perennial springs. Full often wealth cozens the owner. Dainties are spread on his table, but his appetite fails; minstrels wait his bidding, but his ears are deaf to all the strains of music; holidays he may have as many as he pleases, but for him recreation has lost all its charms: or he is young, fortune has come to him by inheritance, and he makes pleasure his pursuit till sport becomes more irksome than work, and dissipation worse than drudgery. Ye know how riches make themselves wings; like the bird that roosts in the tree, they fly away. In sickness and despondency these ample means that once seemed to whisper, "Soul, take thine ease," prove themselves to be poor comforters. In death they even tend to make the pang of separation more acute, because there is the more to leave, the more to lose. We may well say, if we have wealth, "My God, put me not of with these husks; let me never make a god of the silver and the gold, the goods and the chattels, the estates and investments, which in thy providence thou hast given me. I beseech thee, bless me indeed. As for these worldly possessions, they will be my bane unless I have thy grace with them."

And if you have not wealth, and perhaps the most of you will never have it, say, "My Father, thou hast denied me this outward and seeming good, enrich me with thy love, give me the gold of thy favour, bless me indeed; then allot to others whatever thou wilt, thou shalt divide my portion, my soul shall wait thy daily will; do thou bless me indeed, and I shall be content."

Another transient blessing which our poor humanity fondly covets and eagerly pursues is fame. In this respect we would fain be more honourable than our brethren, and outstrip all our competitors. It seems natural to us all to wish to make a name, and gain some note in the circle we move in at any rate, and we wish to make that circle wider if we can. But here, as of riches it is indisputable that the greatest fame does not bring with it any equal measure of gratification. Men, in seeking after notoriety or honour, have a degree of pleasure in the search which they do not always possess when they have gained their object. Some of the most famous men have also be some of the most wretched of the human race. If thou hast honour and fame, accept it; but let this prayer go up, "My God, bless thou me indeed, for what profit were it, if my name were in a thousand mouths, if thou shouldest spue it out of thy mouth? What matter, though my name were written in marble, if it were not written in the Lamb's Book of Life? These blessings are only apparently blessings, windy blessings, blessings that mock me. Give me thy blessing: then the honour which comes of thee will make me blessed indeed." If you happen to live in obscurity, and have never entered the lists for honours among your fellow-men, be content to run well your own course and fulfil truly your own vocation. To lack fame is not the most grievous of ills; it is worse to have it like the snow, that whitens the ground in the morning, and disappears in the heat of the day. What matters it to a dead man that men are talking of him? Get thou the blessing indeed.

There is another temporal blessing which wise men desire, and legitimately may wish for rather than the other two—*the blessing of health*. Can we ever prize it sufficiently? To trifle with such a boon is the madness of folly. The highest eulogiums that can be passed on health would not be extravagant. He that has a healthy body is infinitely more blessed than he who is sickly, whatever his estates may be. Yet if I have health, my bones well set, and my muscles well strung, if I scarcely know an ache or pain, but can rise in the morning, and with elastic step go forth to labour, and can cast myself upon my couch at night, and sleep the sleep of the happy, yet, oh let me not glory in my strength! In a moment it may fail me. A few short weeks may reduce the strong man to a skeleton. Consumption may set in, the cheek may pale with the shadow of death. Let not the strong man glory in his strength. The Lord "delighteth not in the strength of the horse: he taketh not pleasure in the legs of a man." And let us not make are boast concerning these things. Say, thou that are in good of health, "My God, bless me indeed. Give me the healthy soul. Heal me of my spiritual diseases. Jehovah Rophi come, and purge out the leprosy that is in my heart by nature: make me healthy in the heavenly sense, that I may not be put aside among the unclean, but allowed to stand amongst the congregation of thy saints. Bless my bodily health to me that I may use it rightly, spending the strength that I have in thy services and to thy glory; otherwise, though blessed with health, I may not be blessed indeed." Some of you, dear friends, do not possess that great treasure of health. Wearisome days and nights are appointed you. Your bones are become an almanac, in which you note the changes of the weather. There is much about you that is fitted to excite pity. But I pray that you may have the blessing indeed, and I know what that is. I can heartily sympathise with a sister that said to me the other day, "I had such nearness to God when I was sick, such full assurance, and such joy in the Lord, and I regret to say I have lost it now; that I could almost wish to be ill again, if thereby I might have a renewal of communion with God." I have often times looked gratefully back to my sick chamber. I am certain that I did never grow in grace one half so much anywhere as I have upon the bed of pain. It ought not to be so. Our joyous mercies ought to be great fertilizers to our spirit; but not unfrequently our griefs are more salutary than our joys. The pruning knife is best for some of us. Well, after all, whatever you have to suffer, of weakness, of debility, of pain, and anguish, may it be so attended with the divine presence, that this light affliction may workout for you a far more exceeding and eternal weight of glory, and so you may be blessed indeed.

I will only dwell upon one more temporal mercy, which is very precious-I mean *the blessing of home.* I do not think any one can ever praise it too highly, or speak too well of it. What a blessing it is to have the fireside, and the dear relationships that gather round the word "Home," wife, children, father, brother, sister! Why, there are no songs in any language that are more than full of music than those dedicated to "Mother." We hear a great deal about the German "Fatherland"-we like the sound. But the word "Father," is the whole of it. The "land" is nothing: the "Father" is key to the music. There are many of us, I hope, blessed with a great many of these relationships. Do not let us be content to solace our souls with ties that must ere long be sundered. Let us ask that over and above them may come the blessing indeed. I thank thee, my God, for my earthly father; but oh, be thou my Father, then am I blessed indeed. I thank thee, my God, for a mother's love; but comfort thou my soul as one whom a mother comforteth, then am I blessed indeed. I thank thee, Saviour, for the marriage bond; but be thou the bridegroom of my soul. I thank thee for the tie of brotherhood; but be thou my brother born for adversity, bone of my bone, flesh of my flesh. The home thou hast given me I prize, and thank thee for it; but I would dwell in the house of the Lord forever, and be a child that never wanders, wherever my feet may travel, from my Father's house with its many mansions. You can thus be blessed indeed. If not domiciled under the paternal care of the Almighty, even the blessing of home, with all its sweet familiar comforts, does not reach to the benediction which Jabez desired for himself. But do I speak to any here that are separated from kith and kin? I know some of you have left behind you in the bivouac of life graves where parts of your hearts are buried, and that which remains is bleeding with just so many wounds. Ah, well! the Lord bless you indeed! Widow, thy maker is thy husband. Fatherless one, he hath said, "I will not leave you comfortless: I will come to you." Oh, to find all your relationships made up in him, then you will be blessed indeed! I have perhaps taken too long a time in mentioning these temporary blessings, so let me set the text in another light. I trust we have had human blessings and temporary blessings, to fill our hearts with gladness, but not to foul our hearts with worldliness, or to distract our attention away from the things that belong to our everlasting welfare.

Let us proceed, thirdly, to speak of *imaginary blessings*. There are such in the world. From them may God deliver us. "Oh that thou wouldest bless me indeed!" Take the Pharisee. He stood in the Lord's house, and he thought he had the Lord's blessing, and it made him very bold, and he spoke with unctuous self-complacency, "God, I thank thee, that I am not as other men are," and so on. He had the blessing, and well indeed he supposed himself to have merited it. He had fasted twice in the week, paid tithes of all that he possessed, even to the odd farthing on the mint, and the extra halfpenny on the cummin he had used. He felt he had done everything. His the blessing of a quiet or a quiescent conscience; good, easy man. He was a pattern to the parish. It was a pity everybody did not live as he did; if they had, they would not have wanted any police. Pilate might have dismissed his guards, and Herod his soldiers. He was just one of the most excellent persons that ever breathed. He adored the city of which he was a burgess! Ay; but he was not blessed indeed. This was all his overweening conceit. He was a mere wind-bag, nothing more, and the blessing which he fancied had fallen upon him, had never come. The poor publican whom he thought accursed, went to his home justified rather than he. The blessing had not fallen on the man who thought he had it. Oh, let everyone of us here feel the sting of his rebuke, and pray: "Great God, save us from imputing to ourselves a righteousness which we do not possess. Save us from wrapping ourselves up in our own rags, and fancying we have put on the wedding garments. Bless me indeed. Let me have the true righteousness. Let me have the true worthiness which thou canst accept, even that which is of faith in Jesus Christ,"

Another form of this imaginary blessing is found in persons who would scorn to be thought self-righteous. Their delusion, however is near akin. I hear them singing-

"I do believe, I will believe,
That Jesus died for me;
And on his cross he shed his blood,
From sin to set me free."

You believe it, you say, Well, but how do you know? Upon what authority do you make so sure? Who told you? "Oh, I believe it." Yes, but we must mind what we believe. Have you any clear evidence of a special interest in the blood of Jesus? Can you give any spiritual reasons for believing that Christ has set you free from sin? I am afraid that some have got a hope that has not got any ground, like an anchor without any fluke-nothing to grasp, nothing to lay hold upon. They say they are saved, and they stick to it they are, and think it wicked to doubt it; but yet they have no reason to warrant their confidence. When the sons of Kohath carried the ark, and touched it with their hands, they did rightly; but when Uzzah touched it he died. There are those who are ready to be fully assured; there are others whom it will be death to talk of it. There is a great difference between presumption and full assurance. Full assurance is reasonable: it is based on solid ground. Presumption takes for granted, and with brazen face pronounces that to be its own to which it has no right whatever. Beware, I pray thee, of presuming that thou art saved. If with thy heart thou dost trust in Jesus, then thou art saved; but if thou merely sayest, "I trust in Jesus," it doth not save thee. If thy heart be renewed, if thou shalt hate the things that thou didst once love, and love the things that thou didst once hate; if thou hast really repented; if there be a thorough change of mind in thee; if thou be born again, then hast thou reason to rejoice: but if there be no vital change, no inward goodliness; if there be no love to God, no prayer, no work of the Holy Spirit, then thy saying, " I am saved," is but thine own assertion, and it may delude, but it will not deliver thee. Our prayers ought to be, "Oh that thou wouldest bless me indeed, with real faith, with real salvation, with the trust in Jesus that is the essential of faith; not with the conceit that begets credulity. God preserve us from imaginary blessing!" I have meet with persons who said, "I believe I am saved, because I dreamt it." Or, "Because I had a text of scripture that applied to my own case. Such and such a good man said so and so in his sermon." Or "because I took to weeping and was excited, and felt as I never felt before." Ah! But nothing will stand the trial but this, "Dost thou abjure all confidence in everything but the finished work of Jesus and dost thou come to Christ to be reconciled in him to God?" If thou dost not, thy dreams and visions, and fancies, are but dreams, and visions, and fancies, and will not serve thy turn when most thou needest them. Pray the Lord to bless thee indeed, for of that sterling verity in all thy walk and talk there is a great scarcity.

Too much I am afraid, that even those who are saved-saved for time and eternity-need this caution, and have good cause to pray this prayer that they may learn to make a distinction between some things which they think to be spiritual blessings, and others which are blessings indeed. Let me show you what I mean. Is it certainly a blessing to get an answer to a prayer after your own mind? I always like to qualify my most earnest prayer with, "Not as I will, but as thou wilt." Not only ought I to do it, but I would like to do it, because otherwise I might ask for something which it would be dangerous for me to receive. God might give it me in anger, and I might find little sweetness in the grant, but much soreness in the grief it caused me. You remember how Israel of old asked for flesh, and God gave them quails; but while the meat was yet in there mouths the wrath of God came upon them. Ask for the meat, if you like, but always put in this: "Lord, if this is not a real blessing, do not give it me." "Bless me indeed." I hardly like to repeat the old story of the good woman whose son was ill-a little child near death's door-and she begged the minister, a Puritan, to pray for its life. He did pray very earnestly, but he put in, "If it be thy will save this child. The woman said, "I can not bear that: I must have you pray that the child will live. Do not put in any ifs or buts." "Woman," said the minister, "it may be you will live to rue the day that you ever wished to set your will up against God's will." Twenty years later she was carried away in a fainting fit from under Tyburn gallows-tree, where that son was put to death as a felon. Although she had lived to see her child grow up to be a man, it would have been infinitely better for her had the child died, and infinitely wiser had she left it to God's will. Do not be quiet so sure that what you think an answer to prayer is any proof of divine love. It may leave much room for thee to seek unto the Lord, saying, "Oh that though wouldest bless me indeed!" So sometimes great exhilaration of spirit, liveliness of heart, even though it be religious joy, may not always be a blessing. We delight in it and oh, sometimes when we have had gatherings for prayer here, the fire has burned, and our souls have glowed! We felt at the time how we could sing-

> "My willing soul would stay
> In such a frame as this,
> And sit and sing herself away
> To everlasting bliss."

So far as that was a blessing we are thankful for it; but I should not like to set such seasons up, as if my enjoyments are the main token of God's favour; or as if they were the chief signs of his blessing. Perhaps it would be a greater blessing to me to be broken in spirit, and laid low before the Lord at present time. When you ask for the highest joy, and pray to be on the mountain with Christ, remember it may be as much a blessing; yea, a blessing indeed to be brought into the Valley of Humiliation, to be laid very low, and constrained to cry out in anguish, "Lord, save, or I perish!"

> "If to-day he deigns to bless us
> With a sense of pardon'd sin,
> He to-morrow may distress us,
> Make us feel the plague within,
> All to make us
> Sick of self, and fond of him."

These variable experiences of ours may be blessings indeed to us, when, had we been always rejoicing, we might have been like Moab, settled on our lees, and not emptied from vessel to vessel. It fares ill with those who have no changes; they fear not God. Have we not, dear friends, sometimes envied those persons that are always calm and unruffled, and are never perturbed in mind? Well, there are Christians whose evenness of temper deserves to be emulated. And as for that calm repose, that unwavering assurance which comes from the Spirit of God, it is a very delightful attainment; but I am not sure that we ought to envy anybody's lot because it is more tranquil or less exposed to storm and tempest than our own. There is a danger of saying "Peace, peace," where there is no peace, and there is no calmness which arises from callousness. Dupes there are who deceive there own souls. "They have no doubts," they say, but it is because they have little heart searching. They have no anxieties, because they have not much enterprise or many pursuits to stir them up. Or it may be they have no pains, because they have no life. Better go to heaven, halt and maimed, than go marching on in confidence down to hell. "Oh that thou wouldst bless me indeed!" My God, I will envy no one of his gifts or his graces, much less of his inward mood or his outward circumstances, if only thou wilt "bless me indeed." I would not be comforted unless thou comfortest me, nor have any peace but Christ my peace, nor any rest but the rest which cometh from the sweet savour of the sacrfice of Christ. Christ shall be all in all, and none shall be anything to me save himself. O that we might always feel that we are not to judge as to the manner of the blessing, but must leave it with God to give us what we would have, not the imaginary blessing, the superficial and apparent blessing, but the blessing indeed!

Equally too with regard to our work and service, I think our prayer should always be, "Oh that thou wouldst bless me indeed!" It is lamentable to see the work of some good men, though it is not ours to judge them, how very pretentious, but how very unreal it is. It is really shocking to think how some men pretend to build up a church in the course of two or three evenings. They will report, in the corner of the newspapers, that there were forty-three persons convinced of sin, and forty-six justified, and sometimes thirty-eight sanctified; I do not know what besides of wonderful statistics they give as to all that is accomplished. I have observed congregations that have been speedily gathered together, and great additions have been made to the church all of a sudden. And what has become of them? Where are those churches at the present moment? The dreariest deserts in Christendom are those places that where fertilised by the patent manures of certain revivalists. The whole church seemed to have spent its strengh in one rush and effort after something, and it ended in nothing at all. They built there wooden house, and piled up the hay, and made a stubble spire that seemed to reach the heavens, and there fell one spark, and all went away in smoke; and he that came to labour next time-the successor of the great builder-had to get the ashes swept away before he could do any good. The prayer of every one that serves God should be, "Oh that thou wouldst bless me indeed." Plod on, plod on. If I only build one piece of masonry in my life, and nothing more, if it be gold, silver, or precious stones, it is a good deal for a man to do; of such precious stuff as that, to build even one little corner which will not show, is a worthy service. It will not be much talked of, but will last. There is the point: it will last. "Establish thou the work of our hands upon us; yea the work of our hands establish thou it." If we are not builders in an established church, it is of little use to try at all . What God establishes will stand, but what men will build without his establishment will certainly come to nought. "Oh that thou wouldst bless me indeed!" Sunday-school teacher, be this your prayer. Tract distributor, local preacher, whatever you may be, dear brother or sister, whatever your form of service, do ask the Lord that you may not be one of those plaster builders using sham compo that only requires a certain amount of frost and weather to make it crumble to pieces. Be it yours, if you cannot build a cathedral, to build at least one part of the marvellous temple that God is piling for eternity, which will outlast the stars.

I have only one thing more to mention before I bring this sermon to a close. The blessings of God's grace are *blessings indeed*, which in right earnest we ought to seek after. By these marks shall ye know them. Blessings indeed, are such blessings as come from the pierced hand; blessings that come from Calvary's bloody tree, streaming from the Saviour's wounded side-thy pardon, thine acceptance, thy spiritual life: the bread that is meat indeed, the blood that is drink indeed-thy oneness to Christ, and all that comes of it-these are blessings indeed. Any blessing that comes as a result of the Spirit's work in thy soul is a blessing indeed; though it humble thee, though it strip thee, though it kill thee, it is a blessing indeed. Though the harrow go over and over thy soul, and the deep plough cut into thy very heart; though thou be maimed and wounded, and left for dead, yet if the Spirit of God do it, it is a blessing indeed. Anything that he does, accept it; do not be dubious of it; but pray that he might continue his blessed operations in thy soul. Whatsoever leads thee to God is in like manner a blessing indeed. Riches may not do it. There may be a golden wall between thee and God. Health will not do it: even the strength and marrow of thy bones may keep thee at a distance from thy God. But anything that draws thee nearer to him is a blessing indeed. What though it be a cross that raiseth thee? Yet if raise thee to God it shall be a blessing indeed. Anything that reaches into eternity, with a preparation for the world to come, anything we can carry across the river, the holy joy that is to blossom in those fields beyond the swelling flood, the pure cloudless love of the brotherhood which is to be the atmosphere of truth for ever-anything of this kind that has the eternal broad arrow on it-the immutable mark-is a blessing indeed. And anything which helps me to glorify God is a blessing indeed. If I be sick, and that helps me to praise Him, it is a blessing indeed. If I be poor, and I can serve him better in poverty than in wealth, it is a blessing indeed. If I be in contempt, I will rejoice in that day and leap for joy, if it be for Christ's sake-it is a blessing indeed. Yea, my faith shakes off the disguise, snatches the vizor from the fair forehead of the blessing, and counts it all joy to fall into divers trials for the sake of Jesus and the recompense of reward that he has promised. "Oh that we may be blessed indeed!"

Now, I send you away with these three words: "Search." See whether the blessings are blessings indeed, and be not satisfied unless you know that they are of God, tokens of his grace, and earnests of his saving purpose. "Weigh"-that shall be the next word. Whatever though hast, weigh it in the scale, and ascertain if it be a blessing indeed, conferring such grace upon you as causeth you to abound in love, and to abound in every good word and work. And lastly, "Pray." So pray that this prayer may mingle with all thy prayers, that whatsoever God grants or whatever he withholds thou mayest be blessed indeed. Is it a joy-time with thee? O that Christ may mellow thy joy, and prevent the intoxication of earthly blessedness from leading thee aside from close walking with him! In the night of sorrow, pray that he will bless thee indeed, lest the wormwood also intoxicate thee and make thee drunk, lest thy afflictions should make thee think hardly of him. Pray for the blessing, which having, thou art rich to all the intents of bliss, or which lacking, thou art poor and destitute, though plenty fill thy store. "If thy presence go not with me, carry us not up hence." But "Oh that thou wouldest bless me indeed!"

J. OSWALD SAUNDERS

J.Oswald Saunders was born in 1902 in Invercargill, New Zealand. After training as a solicitor, he joined the staff of the New Zealand Bible Training Institute in 1926 as secretary and treasurer.

In 1946 he was appointed home director of the China Inland Mission in Australia. When it was renamed the Overseas Missionary Fellowship in 1954, he had the responsibility of reorganizing the mission after the communist takeover of mainland China.

Himself a great missionary statesman and Bible teacher, he was in constant demand, travelling to many mission stations where he encouraged and enriched the lives of the missionaries with his wealth of spiritual experience and deep knowledge of the Word of God.

Dr. Sanders died on the 24th October 1992 in his native New Zealand, after a brief illness.

A Christian leader for almost seventy years, he wrote more than forty books on spiritual living, including *'Problems of Christian Discipleship'* from which this sermon is taken.

Chapter Three

GOD-SANCTIONED AMBITION

"Enlarge my coast"
1 Chron.4:10.

"And Jabez was more honourable than his brethren: and his mother called his name Jabez, saying, Because I bare him with sorrow. And Jabez called on the God of Israel, saying, Oh that thou wouldest bless me indeed, and enlarger my coast, and that thine hand might be with me, and that thou wouldest keep me from evil, that it may not grieve me! And God granted him that which he requested" (1 Chron.4:9, 10).

"CROMWELL, I charge thee, fling away ambition: by that sin fell the angels." When Shakespeare put these words into the mouth of one of his characters-Cardinal Wolsey-was he giving advice which accords with the teaching of Scripture? Is ambition necessarily a base and selfish quality? It is indeed the "last infirmity of noble minds"?

The Bible appears to teach that there is an ambition which warrants these strictures; but also that there is an ambition which is worthy and to be cherished. In essence, any ambition which centres around and terminates upon oneself is unworthy, while an ambition which has the glory of God as its centre is not only legitimate but positively praiseworthy.

A MASTER AMBITION

Many fail of worthwhile achievement simply because they have no master ambition, no dominating purpose to unify their lives. They live haphazardly and not like Paul, who said, "This one thing I do."

If we are to achieve a worthwhile ambition it will require such a whole hearted abandonment as the orator Demosthenes displayed in pursuit of oratorical power. When Demosthenes first spoke in public he was hissed of the platform. His voice was harsh and weak and his appearance unprepossessing. He determined that his fellow-citizens would yet hang on his words and to this end he gave himself day and night to elocution. He shaved half his head so that he would not be drawn into the vortex of society life. To overcome a stammer he recited with pebbles in his mouth. He matched his orations with the thunder of the Aegean Sea that his voice might gain in volume. An ugly hitching of the shoulder he corrected by standing beneath a suspended sword. He corrected any facial distortions as he practised in front of a mirror. It is not surprising that when he next appeared in public, he moved the nation. He was speaking with another orator on a matter of vital moment to the nation. When his companion concluded his speech the crowed said, "What marvellous oratory!" But when Demosthenes reached his peroration they cried with one voice, "Let us go and fight Philip!"

Worldly ambition expresses itself in three main directions: to build a reputation, to amass wealth, to wield power, but its fatal flaw is that its centre is self and not God. This ambition does not ennoble: it engenders jealousy and envy. It is impatient of the consideration due to others and will go to all lengths to achieve its ends. It drives the "successful" business man to crush ruthlessly his weaker and more scrupulous competitor. But how tawdry and unsubstantial are its rewards and how trivial its achievements when viewed in the light of eternity! The ambition of Napoleon or a Hitler brought them momentary glory, but with it eternal shame. Such an ambition as this is the antithesis of the spirit of the cross of Christ.

AN UNWORTHY AMBITION

It is possible to nurse an unworthy ambition in religious as well as worldly associations. Before there transforming experience at Pentecost, two of our Lord's intimates, James and John used there doting mother in an endeavour to gain them a preferment over their ten brethren. They stooped to pretty intrigue to exclude the other claimants to the places of supreme privilege in Christ's Kingdom. Even the Last Supper was not too sacred an occasion to be marred by their selfish strife. Nor were the ten free from the same unworthy ambition, else why were they so indignant with James and John for forestalling them? They had yet to learn, and by very bitter experience, that the lowliest is the greatest in Christ's Kingdom; but eventually they did master the lesson.

The ambition which God sanctions is far otherwise. The true disciple of Christ lives by an entirely different scale of values. A God-approved ambition must be pure and noble, tinged with self-abnegation and self-sacrifice. The disciples recognises that he belongs to Christ-body, intellect, emotions, and will-and therefore any honour which may come to him belongs to his Master. Like his Lord, he cherishes the ambition to give rather than to receive, to serve rather than to be served, to use his time and talents for his Master rather than to be served, to use his time and talents for his Master than debase them in pursuit of self-aggrandizement.

THE DETERMINING MOTIVE

It is the underlying motive which determines the character of ambition and renders it laudable or unworthy. "Seekest thou great things *for thyself*? Seek them not," was the Lord's message to Baruch (Jer. 45:5). In His memorable Sermon on the Mount Christ counselled, "Lay not up *for yourselves* treasure on earth" (Matt. 6:19). The wrong lies not in the ambition itself but in its inspiring motive. An intensely ambitious man himself, Paul encouraged others to aim high by citing himself as an example. "I press toward the mark for the prize." "So run that ye may obtain." "Study to show thyself approved unto God, a workman needing not to be ashamed." Three of his own unusual ambitions appear-some quiet incidentally-in his epistles: "to be well-pleasing to God" (2 Cor. 5:9), "to be quiet," the quiet of inner response, not of inertia (1 Thess 4:11), and "to preach the gospel where Christ has not been already named" (Rom. 15:20). All his ambitions found their centre in Christ, "that in all things *He* might have the pre-eminence" (Col. 1:18).

David Brainard was so consumed with ambition to glorify Christ by winning souls for His Kingdom that he wrote in his dairy, "I cared not where or how I lived, or what hardship I endured so that I could but gain souls for Christ. While I was asleep I dreamt of such things, and when I walked the first thing I thought of was winning souls to Christ." The supreme ambition of George Whitefield found expression in this tremendous sentence: "If God did not give me souls, I believe I would die."

Here then is the measuring rod for an ambition which is legitimate for the Christian. Is its supreme objective the glory of God and not the glory of the disciple? Will its fulfilment make the disciple more useful in Christ's service and a greater blessing to his fellow-men? Theodore Monod compressed it into this motto: "All in Christ, by the Holy Spirit, for the glory of God."

One of the great Bible examples of holy ambition is found in the passage at the head of this chapter. This brief paragraph affords a remarkable insight into the character and ambitions of the one man who God singled out from among all his contemporaries for honourable mention. It is a remarkable thumbnail sketch which lays bare the ambition which caused him to become "more honourable than his brethren." Its very setting, an oasis in the wilderness of the dead, would indicate the importance that God attached to his attainments. When God troubles to preserve the epitaph of one man out of millions and gives it in such concise and meaningful language, we can be certain that it will repay detailed study.

Before passing to the subject of ambition, two lessons from the life of Jabez are worthy of note.

There is no need for *obscurity to overshadow a life.* Only the bear essentials relevant to the divine purpose are contained in the epitaph of Jabez. No indication was given that he was wealthy, gifted, or even popular-only that he became more honourable than his brethren, and his contemporaries, too, for of him alone does God preserve a record of posterity. Church history teaches that God sometimes takes up obscure men or women and uses them to an extraordinary degree while passing by people of much greater gift. Jabez sprang out of obscurity into age-long prominence because of his secret prayer-life. His prayer provides the key to his life.

God is sympathetic toward a holy ambition. Jabez cherished a strong ambition to which God responded magnificently. His four petitions were indeed ambitious and on the surface might have appeared selfish. But the fact that "God granted him that which he requested" indicates that the glory of God rather than selfish aggrandisement's was his real desire. God does not honour unworthy motives, nor does He answer self-centred prayers. "Ye ask and receive not, because ye ask amiss that ye may consume it upon your lusts" (Jas. 4:3). God delighted to honour Jabez because Jabez desired to honour God. "Them that honour Me, I will honour" is an abiding principle.

The fourfold petition of his prayer voiced the aspiration of his heart.

He plead for *Divine Enrichment.* "Oh that Thou wouldest bless me indeed." No ordinary blessing would satisfy him. He yearned for something which surpassed every previous experience. God's ear is always attentive to such a plea, for a true spiritual blessing always ennobles character and qualifies to bring greater blessing to others. "And God granted him that which he requested."

He prayed for *Divine Enlargement.* "Oh that Thou wouldest enlarge my coast." His primary concern doubtless was, for an increase in territory which would bring him greater influence, but it was not for mere personal aggrandisement, for God granted his request. His was a God-sanctioned ambition. Some of our hymns sound pious but they do not always stand close analysis. They can express a dangerous half-truth. Here is one:

> Content to fill a little space,
> If God be glorified.

That is, of course, a worthy sentiment. We all must be able to glorify God in "a little space" if that is where He has placed us. Until we qualify there, it is unlikely that we will be promoted. But the unintentional implication of this couplet is that God can be glorified more in a little space than in a larger sphere. Should we not be ambitious to fill a larger place if we can thereby bring more glory to God? God does not want all His children filling only the small places of life. He requires those who will serve Him loyally and glorify Him in great positions of responsibility. Such contentment as the hymn envisages could spring from spiritual inertia and an unwillingness to pay the price of occupying larger territory for Christ.

Would not Carey's motto be more to the glory of our Master? "Attempt great things for God. Expect great thing from God." God wants men who, like Jabez, are discontented with a limited opportunity when they could bring greater glory to God in a wider sphere. Our ambition should be for a wider influence for God, a deeper love toward God, a stronger faith in God and a growing knowledge of God. The motive of our ambition must be carefully watched; but when it is right, God will not deny our prayer for an enlarged sphere. "And God granted him that which he requested."

The third petition was for *Divine Enablement*. "Oh that Thine hand might be with me." An enlarged coast involves increasing responsibilities and imposes greater demands. Jabez knew he required a power greater than his own to possess and develop his new territory for God. God's hand represents His mighty power. John the Baptist moved Israel so mightily because "the hand of the Lord was with him" (Luke 1:66). So it was with Jabez, for "God granted him that which he requested."

His final request was for *Divine Environment*. "Oh that thou wouldest keep me from evil, that it may not grieve me." Jabez well knew the inevitable peril of an enlarged coast-increased activity on the part of his enemies. Attempting great things for God always attracts the hostile attentions of the Evil One, and Jabez' prayer is appropriate in all ages. "I pray that Thou wouldest keep me from the Evil one" (John 17:15) was the Lord's petition for His own. We are very vulnerable to his attacks and need to walk in humble dependence on God. In his conscious need Jabez prayed for a sense of God's environing presence, "and God granted him that which he requested."

There is nothing which God will not do for the man whose sole ambition is for His greater glory.

REV. JAMES JOHN EASTWOOD

Rev. James John Eastwood was born on the 22nd April, 1828 at Chatham, Kent. Little is known of the early years of his life and we have no information as to how or when he came to a saving knowledge of Christ.

As a young man he was in business in the town of Norwich and while there he was generally preaching every Sunday. The Rev. Patrick Chatham, who was his minister, convinced him of the desirability of entering the ministry and this led him to apply to Cheshunt College where he was accepted, and remained there five years.

On leaving Cheshunt he was invited to become the minister of Lodgestreet Chapel, in Bristol, staying there just twelve months.

After leaving Lodgestreet he was called to Tyldesley Chapel and spent the next twenty two years as their minister.

He passed away on Saturday 28th June 1879, still in the prime of life, and after a short illness.

His last distinguishable words being
> 'Nothing in my hand I bring,
> Simply to the cross I cling.'

For some years during his ministry he had been in the habit of writing out his sermons in full, thus enabling them to be published. He occasionally contributed sermons and articles to the Gospel Magazine of which Dr. Doudney was editor, and who said of Eastmead, 'It is evident that our brother resorted to the Fountain Head for supply. I believe that none would have felt more tenacious than he, of giving heed to that most solemn injunction, "To the law and to the testimony; if they speak not according to this word, it is because there is no light in them."'

This sermon on the prayer of Jabez was taken from *Sermons by the late Rev. James John Eastwood* which was published in memory of his ministry in 1879, the year of his death.

Chapter Four

THE PRAYER OF JABEZ

☙

"And Jabez called on the God of Israel, saying, Oh that Thou wouldest bless me indeed, and enlarge my coast, and that thine hand might be with me, and that thou wouldest keep me from evil, that it may not grieve me! And God granted him that which he resquested." 1 Chronicles iv.10.

☙

How true is the description which the Word of God gives of men in their nature state, where it says, "Without God in the world" (Ephesians ii.12). We see men live, and perform the duties of the world. They prosper, and everything seems to go on well with them, so far as the things of the present life. But they are *without God in the world.* Nor is this a matter which distresses them. There are thousands of persons in this locality, who are living from day to day, from week to week, and from year to year, in this state, and are quite contented and satisfied with themselves. They are living only for the flesh, and not for the spirit; for time, and not for eternity. But how different is the case with those who are the children of grace. They are not, they cannot be, happy, unless they have a proof of the Divine presence. In all their plans and undertakings, they must be inwardly conscious of having God's presence, or they cannot move one step. We see this illustrated in the case of Jacob, who, when he has left his father's house to go to Pandan-aram, vowed a vow, saying, "If God will be with me, and will keep me in this way that I go, and will give me bread to eat and raiment to put on, so that I come to my father's house in peace: then shall the Lord be my God" (Genisis xxviii. 20,21). Jacob was one who found grace in the eyes of God, and, therefore, he could not go one step in his journey, without being sensible of God's presence. And, when the angel appeared to him, after his departure from Laban, and revealed to Jacob who he was, how he wrestled with that angel of the covenant, and would not let him go. "I will not let thee go," said he, "except thou bless me" (Genesis xxxii. 26). The Lord had blessed Jacob *temporally* during his stay with Laban. He had increased in oxen and asses, flocks, and men servants, and women servants, so that what he had wanted from the angel of the covenant was a *spiritual* blessing-an inward sense of His Divine presence. Take again the cases of Moses as the leader of God's people, Israel. How anxious Moses was to have God with him. "If Thy presence go not with me," he says, "carry us not up hence. For wherein shall it be known here that I and Thy people have found grace in Thy sight? is it not that Thou goest with us? so shall we be separated, I and Thy people, from all the people that are upon the face of the earth" (Exodus xxxiii. 15,16). Nothing would satisfy Moses but God's presence. He knew then that all would be well, and he would feel safe and happy. Now, this has ever been the case with all the living family of God. They have never been satisfied unless God has been sensibly present with them-manifesting Himself to them spiritually, as He does not unto the world. If God see fit to bless them with temporal gifts, well, none receive those gifts with a more grateful heart than they. Yet, temporal gifts are nothing to them, compared with an inward sense of the presence of God. Jabez, the character mentioned in the text, seems to be one who wished to prosper in life, which is quite a natural laudable wish. Indeed, every regenerated man may have a natural wish to prosper in the world, without having a covetous spirit, and without having his heart set upon this world. But Jabez wished not only to prosper temporally, but also spiritually. He was a child of grace, and, therefore, looked not so much at the things which are seen and temporal, but at the things which are not seen and eternal.

"And Jabez called on the God of Israel saying, Oh that Thou wouldest bless me indeed, and enlarge my coast, and that Thine hand might be with me, and that Thou wouldest keep me from evil, that it may not grieve me! And God granted him that which he requested." We shall, with the teaching of the Holy Ghost take these words in there spiritual signification, which will be found to be very expressive to the regenerated spirit.

ONE

Let us look at the *Being* addressed, "And Jabez called on the God of Israel." Israel is the name given to Jacob when he wrestled with God. For the angel said unto him, "Thy name shall be called no more Jacob but Israel: for as a prince hast thou power with God and with men, and hast prevailed" (Genisis xxxii. 28). By the words, God of Israel, is meant the God of Jacob; and in what sense was God the God of Jacob? It was in a sense different from that in which he was the God of Esau. The name, God of Israel, is that which relates to him as a covenant God. Jacob was a type of Christ, who is the Covenant Head of all the children of grace. And, therefore, the Holy Ghost, causing it to be recorded that Jabez called on the God of Israel, shows that he was enlightened on the covenant relation which God sustains to the people of His grace, by a teaching which cometh not from man, but from the Holy Ghost. So that the person who calls on the God of Israel, is one who has been quickened by the spirit of God to a new life; and he sees and feels himself to be most guilty, vile, and unclean. He is made sensible of the burden of sin. The law of God has brought home to his conscience in its spirituality, as a fiery, condemning, killing law, and he inwardly cries "Woe is me, for I perish." This is the state into which the God of Israel brings the Israel of God, and when He brings a poor sinner into this state, then it is, that He causes him to call on the God of Israel. It is not possible for an unregenerate man to call on the God of Israel. He may call upon God the creator, which thousands do; but only they whom grace enlightens and teaches to call on the God of Israel, are heard. So that this calling of the God of Israel, is not that which springs from the creature, but from grace working in man. (1) To call on the God of Israel, then, is to call on Him as a gracious God, and such is the character in which He reveals Himself to His people. For, when the Lord passed by before Moses, He proclaimed, "The Lord, the Lord God, merciful and gracious, long-suffering, and abundant in goodness and truth: keeping mercy for thousands, forgiving iniquity, and transgression, and sins" (Exodus xxxiv. 6,7). God hath always dealt with His people as a gracious God, for while He saith He will "by no means clear the guilty," He saith, "He hath not beheld iniquity in Jacob, neither hath He seen perverseness in Israel" (Numbers xxiii. 21). All the living family of God are enabled, by grace, to call on God as gracious; for as soon as they are raised from the dead, and brought to believe in Christ, it is given to them to taste that the Lord is gracious. They feel that they need God to be gracious to their souls, every moment they live. They cannot claim one gift from God, they have such a feeling of indwelling guilt, and such a sense of their vileness before God; and, therefore, they are taught by the spirit of God to call on God as the God of Israel, in other words, that God will be gracious to their souls. (2) To call on the God of Israel, is to call on him as a *sin pardoning* God. For He pardons all the sins of Israel. The pardon of sin is that which was once for all obtained by Christ as the Head of His people, when He was delivered as a sacrifice for sin. This truth is that which the spirit of God reveals to the spiritual understanding of His people, from the time that He causes them to be distressed on account of sin, and not a day passes but they have to call on Him as a sin pardoning God. Sin is not a mere name with them, but an inward, active principle, which is ever at work, disturbing their peace; and, therefore, they feel constant need to call on the God of Israel, to give them a sweet and precious sense of the pardon of their sin through faith in the blood of the Lamb slain. (3) To call on the God of Israel is to call on Him as a *Father*, and this is the relation which all those sustain to God, who have given to them the spirit of adoption. It is a relation which they do not naturally sustain, but that which is bestowed on them by grace, and they sustain it by virtue of their eternal union to Christ, their Covenant Head. And, therefore, all through their pilgrimage, grace causes them to call upon their Father for the supply of their every spiritual need. And, as poor helpless, needy children, they feet constant need to call upon the God of Israel, who is their Father. They want continual supplies of grace. They want their spirits refreshed, and fed with the living bread which cometh down from heaven. They want their spiritual limbs strengthened every moment, or they would fall down helpless, and unable to rise; and, therefore, it is no occasional thing for them, like Jabez, to call on the Lord God of Israel. It seems a very easy thing for men to call on God. The words are soon expressed, and thousands of persons do call on God, whose call springs from the creature; but to call on the God of Israel, in that which belongs not to the creature; but to those who are the Israel of God. The Holy Ghost saith (see Romans x. 13), "Whosoever call upon the name of the Lord shall be saved." Many will read these words as though it is a matter which rests with the free will of the creature. But we will read in the next verse, "How then shall they call on Him in whom they have not believed." And in saving belief is of God, which He gives to His people Israel. Thus, if by the inward teaching of the Holy Ghost, we are conscious that we belong to the Israel of God, the people of His grace, whom God hath made new creatures in Christ Jesus, the word of the text, "And Jabez called on the God of Israel," will be full of spiritual meaning.

TWO

Notice, in the next place, the *request* made. There are several things contained in the request. We shall take them seriatim, in their spiritual signification. (1) The first thing mentioned, is, "Oh that Thou wouldest bless me indeed." Much is involved in the *blessing* of the God of Israel. God has always blessed the people of His grace. The Lord said to Abram, when He called him to depart from his country, "I will bless thee, and make thy name great, and thou shalt be a blessing" (Genesis xii. 2). And this promise, the Lord several times repeats to Abram. And when God gave the covenant of the works to Israel, at Sinai, He said unto them, by the mouth of Moses, "In all places where I record my name I will come unto thee, and I will bless thee" (Exodus xx. 24). And at another time, "The Lord spake unto Moses, saying, Speak unto Aaron and unto his sons, saying, On this wise ye shall bless the children of Israel, saying unto them, The Lord bless thee, and keep thee: the Lord make His face shine upon thee, and be gracious unto thee: the Lord lift up His countenance upon thee, and give thee peace" (Numbers vi. 22-26). To bless, is to make happy. And this is what God makes all the people of His grace. He blesses them not because they are worthy of His blessing. From the moment that God, in His grace, calls them to Himself, the feeling of their heart is that expressed by Israel, when he said, "I am not worthy of least of all the mercies, and of all the faithfulness (truth), which Thou hast shewed unto Thy servant" (Genesis xxxii. 10). God blesses them because He is pleased to make them the people of His choice. He begins to bless a man, when He brings him out of nature's darkness, as one feeling himself blind, into the marvellous light of the Gospel. From that time, the never-ceasing desire of his heart, to the God of Israel, is, "Oh that Thou wouldest bless me." Mark! the little word *"indeed."* We take this to mean, that the blessing craved, was not merely temporal blessing, but a spiritual one, and, therefore, Jabez saith, "Oh that Thou wouldest bless me indeed." The regenerated man is not indifferent to temporal wants and comforts. He has fleshly wants, in common with all men. But one thing, for which he craves above everything else, is to be blessed by the God of Israel-to be blessed in the highest sense, to be blessed spiritually. But when may it be said that the God of Israel blesses a man, spiritually? (1) When He teaches him the mysteries of the kingdom of God, even the mysteries of the everlasting covenant of grace, which are hid from the wise and the prudent, those who are wise in their own eyes. These mysteries are a source of sweet comfort to the believer. His spirit daily sucks from the breasts of the covenant, that milk of grace that satisfies every spiritually longing, and causes him to say, Blessed is that man to whom it is given to know the mysteries of the kingdom of God. (2) God blesses a man when He gives to him *a sweet sense of pardoning love.* And this is that which the believer has, when grace brings a bleeding Christ near to him, and gives him eyes of faith to see him as his sin-atoning Saviour. This sweet sense of pardoning love is, indeed, most precious to the heaven-born spirit. It is to him *an inward evidence* that God hath set His love upon him, that He loves him with covenant, everlasting love. (3) God blesses a man when He causes him to *grow in grace.* And this is that for which the regenerate man longs. He cannot be happy, unless conscious of growing in grace. It is not enough for him to know that God hath once bestowed His grace upon him; not enough to know that he hath experienced the quickening grace of the Holy Ghost; but he wants to grow in grace. He wants to experience a great inflow of that grace, treasured up in Christ for his people, into his spirit. Then it is, he has the inward evidence that God blesses him. And the child of God will not be satisfied, unless he have this inward evidence. If he have it not, he will go about groaning in the spirit, to Him who alone can read the thoughts of his inmost soul, saying, "Oh that Thou wouldest bless me indeed." That which causes him so often to be down in the valley, and troubled by reason of unbelief, is that he wants to feel himself growing in grace, he wants to go on unto perfection. If God were to see fit to bless him with *temporal* prosperity, and grant him all that the carnal mind could desire, he would not, he could not, be satisfied, he would not deem himself blessed indeed. He is truly blessed, whom God causes to grow in grace.

2. Another thing mentioned in the request, which Jabez made to the God of Israel, was, that his *coast* might be enlarged. The word, *coast*, signifies the whole country, within certain limits. The *spiritual interpretation* of these words is very expressive. The true Christian, as an heir of the heavenly inheritance, is ever longing to have his spiritual coast enlarged. At no period in his pilgrimage can he say that it is large enough. All the while he remains in the flesh, his coast will be limited. (1) His *love* is limited. It is that which is intended to grow. The love kindled in the heart, is like the fire on the Jewish altar, of which it is said, "The fire shall ever be burning upon the altar; it shall never go out" (Leviticus vi. 13). But though it is never allowed to go out, yet how often he feels that he wants his

coast enlarged. He wants his love to Christ increased, his love to the brethren of Christ increased, and, therefore, he is constrained to say, "Oh for the grace to fan the spark into a flame." (2) His *faith* is limited. God deals to every man, whom He brings into the kingdom of grace, that measure of faith that pleaseth Him. Hence the living family of God, have not all the same measure of faith. Some have very strong faith, others have but a very small grain, just enough to feel their interest in the blood and righteousness of Christ, and sometimes scarcely sufficient for that, and they are, consequently, led to call on the God of Israel, and say, "Oh that Thou wouldest enlarge our coast, and grant unto us an increase of faith." But, however great the measure of faith which God hath seen fit to deal to any of His living family, it is limited, and therefore, there will always be a desire to have that measure increased. The immortal spirit of grace often feels, when experiencing the upward drawings of the Spirit of God, that it would fain go beyond its limited coast. (3) His *hope* is limited. The Christian's hope is indeed a glorious hope. It is not like the hypocrite's hope, which shall perish, but is the lively, living hope of one who has been begotten again, by a spiritual resurrection, from his dead state. But how feeble his hope is sometimes felt. He can scarcely regard himself as being in that state, in which he is "Looking for that blessed hope, even the glorious appearing of that great God and our Saviour Jesus Christ" (Titus ii. 13). Sometimes the tempter leads him to question, whether the flukes of his anchor are quite safe, and whether, after all, he has not a false hope, and in this state he is constrained to call upon the God of Israel, "Oh that Thou wouldest enlarge my coast," and give to me a hope which extends beyond the coast of earth, but which entereth into that within the veil, whither the forerunner is for us entered, even Jesus our great High Priest (Hebrews vi. 19,20). (4) His *joy* is limited. "These things have I spoken unto you," saith Jesus to His disciples, "that my joy might remain in you, and that your joy might be full" (John xv. 11). The Christian does indeed partake of Christ's joy, and at some favoured times in his history, it is experienced to be a joy which is unspeakable, and full of glory. But those times and seasons are rare. When grace causes him to experience such a season, it has such an influence upon him, as to lead him to say, "Oh that

Thou wouldest enlarge my coast," and give to me an increase of spiritual joy. (5) And, then, we might remark, that the believer's *knowledge* is limited. His knowledge of God, of Christ, of the Scriptures, and of the spiritual things of God, is very limited, and in this sense he often desires that his coast might be enlarged. And thus, how expressive is this request of Jabez, taken in its spiritual signification. It is a request which every child of God is ever making, for his new spirit of grace will never be satisfied while in the flesh. It soars on high-it looks beyond its limited boundary-it stretches away in the bosom of Christ by faith, in to eternity.

3. Another thing mentioned in the request, is, "That Thine hand might be with me." What more can a child of God wish than to have the hand of God with him? The idea supposes the God of Israel to be with him, guiding his every step, shaping his destiny, and ordering all things, according to His own purpose and will, that He may accomplish in him, that which He hath spoken. For, concerning every one of His chosen vessels of mercy, the God of Israel hath spoken to His Eternal Son, words of peace, which He stands engaged to fulfil in their individual experience. The words, "hand of God," are often used in the Holy Scriptures, and are very expressive. To give an instance, or two, we read in 1 Samuel v. 11, that among the Philistines who retained the Ark of God for a time, there was a deadly destruction throughout all the city; the hand of God was very heavy there. In Ezra vii. 9, we read that, "The good hand of God was upon Ezra." When Nehemiah came to Jerusalem, and saw the city in ruins, and the wall broken down, we read, ii. 18, "Then I told them of the hand of my God which was good upon me." And Job saith, "The hand of God hath touched me" (Job xix. 21). And addressing believers, the apostle Peter (1 Peter v. 6) saith, "Humble yourselves under the mighty hand of God." Thus the expression put into the mouth of Jabez, "That Thine hand might be with me," is full of meaning in the mouth of a regenerated man. This is the desire of his heart, every day, every moment, he lives. But for the hand of God being with him, the evil beasts would soon increase upon him. The carnal mind, sin, and the devil, would soon devour him. The secret of his spiritual strength is, that he has the hand of his covenant God

with him. It was that hand which first brought him out of nature's bondage; out of the horrible pit, and the miry clay. It was that hand which brought him to the cross, as a poor, guilty, helpless wretch, and when there, opened his eyes, and gave him not only sight to see the bleeding Lamb of God, but also gave him strength of sight to look at Him. It was that hand which set his feet firm upon a rock of grace, and established his goings in the way of grace, and put a new song in his mouth, even praise unto our covenant God. Indeed, every step which the believer takes, is by the hand of God. Has he faith in the blood and righteousness of Christ? It is the hand of God which gives it to him. Is he exhorted to fight the good fight of faith? It is the hand of God that fights for him. Is he exhorted to humble himself under the mighty hand of God? It is the mighty hand of God which humbles him. Is he exhorted to resist the devil? It is the hand of God that gives him power to resist. Is he exhorted not to be conformed to this world, but transformed by the renewing of his mind? It is the hand of God, working according to His mighty power, which conforms him to the image of Christ, and daily, and hourly, renews his spirit with supplies of grace. And thus, every step which the believer takes in his pilgrimage, is by the hand of the God of Israel, his covenant God. Without that hand, all the exhortations addressed to believers are meaningless, for the living family of God, as a family, are weakness itself. They live, and are upheld, and they walk as seeing Him, who is invisible, because of the hand of God being with them. And the true believer will not be satisfied, unless he experience the hand of God working with him. In other words, he will not be satisfied, unless he experience the Spirit of God working within him, and showing to him the depravity and corruption of his nature, revealing Christ to him with increasing power and sweetness to his heart. He will not be satisfied, unless he experience the spirit of God drawing him upwards above the world-above the flesh, and making his dwelling-place on high. And thus, every prayer which the true Christian offers-every sigh which he sends forth to his covenant God, is, "Oh that Thine hand might be with me." "With me," every moment of my pilgrimage, asleep, awake, at home, abroad, wherever I am, whatever I am doing, and when I come to die, "Oh that Thine hand might be with me."

4. Another thing contained in the request is, "That Thou wouldest keep me from evil." This is a request which the child of God never ceases to make. In the world, he lives in the midst of evil. He has within him an evil heart, and the great evil spirit goeth about as a roaring lion, seeking whom he may devour. So that he needs to be kept from evil. As soon as the Lord, in His grace, quickens a man to life, and causes him to see and feel the evil of his own heart, He makes him to know that he needs to be kept from evil. And, if what the Lord has graciously taught me of my own heart, be any guide, in speaking of the Lord's living family of grace, sure I am that unless everyone of that family be specially and miraculously kept, evil will overcome them. It requires as great a miracle to keep the new hidden man of the heart from evil, as it does to quicken him to life. Much, therefore, is contained in the words, "Keep me from evil." It supposes special power put forth by the God of Israel, on behalf of His people. It belongs to the Holy Ghost, the third person in the Trinity, to keep them. He undertook to do so in the everlasting covenant of grace, and the experience of every poor, tempted, tried believer, is that he is kept. Why is it that the believer, during ten, twenty, thirty, fifty, or more years, it may be, though conscious of much weakness, much in-dwelling sin, many fallings away, many a time crucifying the Son of God afresh, and putting Him to an open shame-why is it that he still knows that he has an interest in Christ? still knows, to the joy of his heart, and the rejoicing of his spirit, that Christ is precious? still knows that covenant blood and covenant blessings are for him? Why is it? Simply, because he has been kept from evil, kept by the power of God through faith, and he shall be kept until his salvation shall be revealed, before an assembled world.

"Saints by the power of God are kept,
Till the salvation come;
We walk by faith as strangers here,
Till Christ shall call us home."

But the reason why Jabez wished that he might be kept from evil is, as he says, "That it may not grieve me." If the child of grace were not kept from evil, it would grieve him-greatly grieve him-for he never can *love evil*; impossible, because he is dead to it by the cross of Christ. Whenever he is laid away by the carnal mind, and is brought into bondage by some evil, some besetting sin, it grieves him. His new spirit of grace is troubled in consequence. And often, the believer is grieved by a sense of in-dwelling sin, and always will be. True, he does not live in sin. His life is strictly moral. He lives unspotted from the world. Yet, his sense of in-dwelling sin, that which distinguishes the child of God from the Pharisee, grieves him, often grieves him; and he would have good cause to question his eternal sonship, if it did not grieve him. How, then, can we justify the request of Jabez, "That evil may not grieve me?" In this way. On the one hand, evil cannot but grieve the child of God, and he knows that it dwells within him; on the other hand, since grace causes him to see himself in Christ, his Covenant Head, as free from evil, and complete in Him, evil does not grieve him, for he knows that when the body of sin is put off, then farewell to evil for ever; and, therefore, the prayer, "That Thou wouldest keep me from evil, that it may not grieve me," in the mouth of the child of God, must be associated with Christ, in order to be explained. Indeed, everything that grace causes the believer to think, and say, and do, is associated with Christ, for He has been eternally united to Him. Christ and He are one, and always will be. So that this request, "That Thou wouldest keep me from evil, that it may not grieve me," will be the established prayer of his daily life. If he were not kept-if one moment he were allowed to fall into evil, it is sure to grieve him, and to pierce him through with many sorrows.

THREE

The answer given to the request. "And God granted him that which he requested." From this we conclude, that his request was indited by the Spirit of God. He it was that put the prayer in the heart of Jabez. No prayer but that which the Spirit of God raises in the heart of a man, is granted by God. How does God make it known to His people, that He has granted their request? In the case of

Jabez, it would require his life-time for God to grant him his request. Would God keep him in suspense, and yet go on answering his prayer in his experience? No. God would make known to him, inwardly, or perhaps by a vision, that He had granted his request, meaning that God would fulfil, in his experience, that which he wished. And so Jabez, as all the children of grace, would have to live by faith on his covenant God that He would be faithful. And we must not think that this request was only once offered, and that then it would pass from the mind of Jabez as a thing of the past. Judging from God's dealings with all His family of grace, he would have offered it many a time before the Lord saw it fit to give him an inward assurance that He had granted his request. Those prayers, which are created within us by the Spirit of God, are not of momentary growth. They do not come by fits and starts, not by impulse, but they come with such soul agony. The Spirit of God lays the request upon the heart and conscience, and it is a relief to the soul to breathe forth to heaven its agonising request. This seems to be the meaning of the blessed Lord's words, which He uttered in reply to one who asked Him, "Lord, are there few that be saved?" He said, "Strive to enter in at the strait gate" (Luke xiii. 23,24). Many, who know nothing of the powers of the world to come, understanding the Lord to mean creature striving, or, as the word means, "agonising." But none but he who has been born from above, and upon whose spirit the Holy Ghost lays some request to make to God, knows what the Lord means. And it often happens, that the Lord lays a request upon His people's spirit for a long time. What soul agony they have to pass through, in urging the desire created in them by the Spirit of God. Often, while communing with God, it may be while on the high road, or while engaged in the pursuits of life, they are conscious of their spirit wrestling with God. The time when God is pleased to bring a sinner out of nature's darkness, when He shows him his sin, and causes him to feel increasing guilt, what is the request which the Holy Ghost lays upon his heart? It is for *mercy*. This request is not an impulsive sort of request, made only once, and done with, so that it becomes a thing of the past, but the Lord sometimes sees fit to lay that request upon his spirit for years, before He reveals Christ in him, as his sin-atoning Saviour. During that time, conviction of sin will be deepened, and deepened, and, consequently, the spiritual agony through which he has to pass, in making his request for mercy, will increase. Thus, when it is said of a child of God, "And God granted him that which he requested," that request originated from God, and was made, time after time, day after day, month after month, year after year, aye, and often made with tears and groans. Ah! It is by bringing those persons, built up in their own creature religion, to this touchstone of spiritual experience, that they are silenced. They know nothing of grace-created prayer. They can talk of going to a throne of grace, as though it were a bodily act, but they know nothing of that spiritual heart-felt prayer, which belongs only to the true Israel of God.

"Prayer is the spirit's breath in man,
Returning whence it came."

JOHN RAVEN

John Raven was born on July 24th 1850 of godly parents who were both members of the Church at Zion Chapel, Leicester, where the late Grey Hazlerigg was then pastor.

It was at the age of 18 that the Lord began to convict him of his sins and within three years he came to a saving knowledge of Christ.

In 1918 he was called to pastor the work at Ebenezer Chapel, Smallfield along with the Church at Hope Chapel, Shaw's Corner, Redhill. This began a happy relationship between pastor and people which was to last over 35 years.

His ministry was very often searching and perceptive, sometimes his discourses had a more doctrinal note, but he always seemed to have most liberty when the text laid on his mind more particularly spoke of the Person and work of the Lord Jesus Christ, and His exaltation at the right hand of the Father. He was a sound Trinitarian. This sermon on the prayer of Jabez is taken from the book *'Sermons by John Raven Vol.II'*.

Chapter Five

JABEZ'S PRAYER

"And Jabez was more honourable than his brethren; and his mother called his name Jabez, saying, Because I bare him with sorrow. And Jabez called on the God of Israel, saying, O that thou wouldest bless me indeed, and enlarge my coast, and that Thine hand might be with me, and that Thou wouldest keep me from evil, that it may not grieve me! And God granted him that which he requested." (1 Chronicles 4: 9-10).

This is a very sweet passage, occurring as it does in a chapter that otherwise consists exclusively of scores of names. In what promises to be a chapter very dull in the reading, one suddenly comes across this beautiful passage in reference to Jabez. It is the only thing we are told about Jabez in the Scriptures, but what an honourable mention it is! We read, first of all, that, "Jabez was more honourable than his brethern: and his mother called his name Jabez, saying, because I bare him with sorrow." Although she bare him with sorrow, yet she had more reasons to rejoice in this son Jabez than in all her other children, for he "was more honourable than his brethren." He was evidently the best of the family. We have known families where the Lord has taken just one of the family and called him or her by His grace, and left the rest in nature's darkness to fill up the measure of their iniquity. What distinguished favour this is! And the one so favoured will take no credit to himself; he will readily say with the poet,

"What was there in me that could merit esteem,
Or give the Creator delight?
'Twas even so Father, we ever must sing,
Because it seemed good in Thy sight."

I knew of one who was such a case as I have mentioned, one called out of a very ungodly family; and yet in speaking of the merciful kindness of the Lord to her, she would speak of herself as the least worthy of all the family. She saw in herself a degree of unworthiness that she could not perceive in the others. Of course, she knew her own heart, and she did not know their hearts; and we may learn from this 9th verse, that the end of a thing is better than the beginning of it. Jabez's mother bare him with sorrow, and certainly in spiritual things there is a more or less sorrowful beginning. The beginning of it is manifest in sorrow of heart, but O, what a merciful sorrow it is! What a merciful affliction it is that is a means of driving the soul to the good Physician! When a man feels his lost condition, his consciousness of his lost condition makes him prize the Saviour, and seek the Lord's face.

Well, we are told of Jabez that he "called on the God of Israel." Mr. Hart, in his beautiful hymn on this passage, says,

"Had he to any other prayed,
To us it had not mattered what."

"Jabez called on the God of Israel." Just look at this for a moment or two. "The God of Israel." You remember how Jacob came to have the name of Israel given to him. It was at the ford Jabbok, when he had sent all his party over the river and he remained alone. There wrestled with him a man till the breaking of the day. We are told that the man touched the hollow of Jacob's thigh so that the sinew shrank, and Jacob halted upon his thigh, but strength was given to him to wrestle. The man said, "Let me go, for the day breaketh.

And he said, I will not let thee go, except Thou bless me," and we
are told, "He blessed him there." And the Lord said, "Thy name
shall be called no more Jacob, but Israel: for as a prince thou hast
power with God and with men, and has prevailed." Now you see
the force of the word here, the "God of Israel." Jabez called on the
God of Israel, that God who hears prayer, who suffers, and indeed
enables, poor people to wrestle with Him by prayer. Not only does
He suffer it, but He gives power to do it. O, if we have grace to
wrestle with God in prayer, it is His merciful gift.

"Prayer is the breath of God in man,
Returning whence it came:
Love is the sacred fire within
And prayer the rising flame."

"Jabez called on the God of Israel," the God who is the Author of
all real prayer, and the Hearer of all sincere prayer. He suffers himself
to be overcome by the importunate, wrestling prayer of poor people.
You remember in the Song of Solomon the Lord says, "Turn away
thine eyes from Me, for they have overcome Me." "Thou hast
ravished My heart with one of thine eyes." O, the Lord is greatly
taken with the desires and the trembling petitions of poor people;
He suffers Himself to be overcome, as the Lord Jesus suffered
Himself to be overcome by the Syrophenecian woman. Although
He seemed to set her back, seemed to hold out no hope of any success
in her petition, but rather rebuffed her, yet she turned what seemed
to be a rebuff into a plea, and the Lord graciously suffered Himself
to be overcome. We might therefore apply the word, "Turn away
thine eyes from Me, for they have overcome Me." Thus the woman
got her will, she got her petition, and so Jabez called upon the God
of Israel.

What a mercy it is that there is a God who hears and answers
prayer, and what a mercy it is to know that God; so to know Him as,
like Jabez, to call upon His name; like Daniel, to set one's face to
seek the Lord by prayer and supplication. "Jabez called on the God
of Israel." "He that cometh to God must believe that He is." Then
Jabez, since he came to Him, since he called upon the God of Israel,

must have believed that He is, or he would not have called upon Him, he would not have come. "Without faith it is impossible to please Him; for he that cometh to God must believe that He is, and that He is a rewarder of them that diligently seek Him." So, Jabez called on the God of Israel, saying, O that Thou wouldest bless me indeed."

Here is the first clause of his petition, "O that Thou wouldest bless me indeed." In the reading, (2 Samuel 7) I noticed David's words, "With *Thy* blessing let the house of Thy servant be blessed forever," and pointed out that it was not any sort of blessing that David would be content with, but it must be the special blessing of God. So here, "O that Thou wouldest bless me indeed." The man wanted a real blessing, a substantial blessing; he was not satisfied with bubbles; he was not satisfied with those things that perished with the using, with things that merely please and pamper the flesh; he wanted a blessing that would do his soul eternal good. "O that Thou wouldest bless me indeed:" and is it not a great thing for God to bless a sinner? Is it not a great thing for God to bless one who deserves to be cursed? It is a wonderful thing, a *wonderful* thing for man, who by reason of his sinfulness and his sins deserves the curse of God, to be enabled to call on the God of Israel and say, "O that Thou wouldest bless me indeed." There is a way whereby God is able to bless a sinner; I say, *He is able to bless a sinner.* You remember it was said to Abraham, "In thy seed shall all the nations of the earth be blessed;" and again in the Psalms it is said of Christ, "And men shall be blessed in Him." This blessing, then, is in and through Jesus Christ; it is for the sake of His name, on the ground of what He has accomplished, on the ground of what He is, on the ground of His precious blood and His all-sufficient and everlasting righteousness that God is able to bless a sinner. "O that Thou wouldest bless me indeed." And you remember that the Psalmist, when he is calling upon his soul to bless the Lord, and calling upon all his inward power to bless and praise the name of the Lord, begins with this: "Who forgiveth all thine iniquities." He speaks of the first and foremost of all the blessings that God bestowed upon him, and indeed a blessing that has every other blessing wrapped up in it. If my sins are pardoned, then I can lack no good thing; if my sins are forgiven, then all that is really good, and all that I need to make me blest in time and throughout eternity, is mine, wrapped up in that great blessing, the forgiveness of sins. So in praying that he might be blessed indeed, Jabez was first of all intent upon the pardon of his sins. O, where are the people who are intent upon getting that from the Lord, the pardon of their sins? The pardon of my sins? Some will say, 'Why, I have no sins.' There are many people who do not stop to think whether they have any sins or not; they are utterly indifferent as to that matter: and if you speak to them about their need of forgiveness, they receive your testimony with scorn. They need no forgiveness. 'I have always lived a good life, I have always done my duty, I have paid my way, I have done this and that; at any rate, I am not so bad as a good many people.' There is no sense of their need of forgiveness; but evidently Jabez felt his need of pardon, and no blessing could really come to him, no real blessing but the way of forgiving love. "O that Thou wouldest bless me indeed." You remember one of our hymns very beautifully says,

"Blest with the pardon of her sin,
My soul beneath Thy shade would lie,
And sing the love that took me in,
While others sank in sin to die."

The Psalmist says too, "Blessed is the man whose transgression is forgiven, whose sin is covered. Blessed is the man unto whom the Lord imputeth not iniquity and in whose spirit there is no guile." O then, this is the blessing that an awakened sinner's heart will be intent upon; a sinner convinced of his sin by the Holy Ghost will be intent upon this blessing. This is what he must have. "For Thy name's sake, O Lord, pardon mine iniquity, for it is great." And when a man gets it, when the Holy Ghost bears witness with the blood of Christ that a man's sins are forgiven him, O the bliss of it! The bliss of it! O what peace, what blessedness, what a sense of divine love flows into the soul when a man is blessed with the forgiveness of his sins. There is something of heaven in it. One says, "'Tis the rich gift of love divine." The bliss of it is known by tasting. You can know nothing of the bliss of it by mere hearsay, hearing the minister or some other person talk about the forgiveness of sins. Reading about it in our hymns or in the Scriptures will give you no just idea of the blessedness of a blood-bought pardon - it must be known and felt. And this is the blessing that Jabez was intent upon. "O that Thou wouldest bless me indeed." He knew, and every spirit taught soul is brought to know this, that if he could get this blessing then all would be well. If you know what it is to receive pardon, then you know what it is to have a blood-purged conscience; to have the blessed assurance, "Then was I in His eyes as one that found favour." "O that Thou wouldest bless me indeed." This blessing must come from the Lord Himself, the Lord only can seal it upon the heart. No word I can utter can convey it, no lips of mere man can convey it to a sinner's soul, it must be by the witness of the Holy Spirit as He bears witness to the atoning blood of the Lord Jesus; and how blessedly He does it! Here is a poor sinner, loaded with guilt, filled with despair because of his actual and original pollution. His appears a hopeless case; and then the blessed Spirit of God comes in with the blood of Christ, with the love of Christ, and opens to him the meaning of such Scriptures as this, "For when we were yet without strength, in due time Christ died for the ungodly." "While we were yet sinners, Christ died for us." "Christ Jesus came into the world to save sinners; of whom I am chief." As the Spirit of God unveils the grace of these Scriptures, O what a vista of heavenly, saving grace is revealed in the heart and conscience! What unspeakable blessedness it brings into the heart to realise forgiveness! It will make the heart melt in love before the Lord, and how the soul will want to be His! "O Lord, truly I am Thy servant; I am Thy servant, and the son of Thine handmaid: Thou hast loosed my bonds." "O that Thou wouldest bless me indeed."

Then the next thing is, "and enlarge my coast." You know the Israelite in those days often possessed only a portion of his inheritance because of the Canaanites that were in the land. Until he dispossessed the Canaanites, he could not enter fully into possession of his inheritance: and so it often happened that a portion of the inheritance was still in the hands of the Canaanites. Well, Jabez prayed that God would enlarge his coast. Now, does that not illustrate for us the case of a child of God who has not entered yet into the full possession of his inheritance? "There remaineth yet very much land to be possessed," but there are these Canaanites. There is, for instance, the power of indwelling sin, there is the working of the flesh, and there is all the vile working of the devil, who, "as a roaring lion walketh about, seeking whom he may devour." By reason of all these things a child of God may often be much straitened; and he does not often enjoy that full assurance that he longs for. His hope is a trembling sort of hope; he has a good many shakings about it; he is not able to come to any certain conclusion as to his standing and his safety; and yet he is not without hope. There is a little hope, like a tiny shoot springing up from the soil: "First the blade, then the ear, after that the full corn of ear," we read. A man's hope may be just like the first coming of the tiny shoot from the earth. Jabez prayed that the Lord would enlarge his coast. The hymn-writer says,

> "And give my straitened bosom room,
> To credit what the promise saith,
> And wait till Thy salvation come."

O, how you need the Lord to work for you against these Canaanitish enemies of yours, this indwelling of sin, this working of the devil who finds so much to work on in your wretched heart, and also the allurements of this world, the many enticing things that are dangled before your eyes. All these hamper the soul so that it is constrained to say, "Enlarge my coast." There is the power of unbelief! O what an enemy of the peace of God's people is unbelief? The hymn-writer says something like this,

> "Break of our legal chains, O God,
> And let our souls go free."

O how a child of God does need to be delivered from the spirit of unbelief and legality which so holds him in bondage, that expectation of being something bettered in himself which prevents him from venturing as a poor, vile sinner, who can do nothing at all, upon a complete and able and willing Saviour. Philpot, I think, described it as "like leaping overboard in a storm" to venture upon Christ, and yet it is only thus venturing that a man experiences the enlarging of his coast, when he is enabled to make that great venture of a naked sinner upon Christ and Christ alone. "Enlarge my coast;" that is, lead me into that fair land of gospel liberty. Do you sometimes thing of the liberty of the gospel with a longing in your heart to be lead into it? You feel to know so little about it, if anything; and at the most, all you can speak of is a kind of Pisgah-like view of it: as Moses viewed the promise land but was not aloud to enter into it, so you may have had a view of the land of gospel liberty, but you have not entered into it yet. "O that Thou wouldest . . . enlarge my coast," lead me into the liberty of Thine own sons and daughters, the liberty wherewith Christ makes His people free, the liberty spoken of in Romans chapter eight: "There is therefore no condemnation to them which are in Christ Jesus." "O that Thou wouldest bless me indeed, and enlarge my coast." Deliver me from all contractions, from all those things that do so straiten me and so hold in bondage, and bring me so much disquietness of heart!

"And that Thine hand might be with me." He felt the need of his God to be with him because he was weak and utterly insufficient. Now is that your feeling and your exercise; that you are so weak, that unless the hand of God is with you, you are in a helpless, hopeless case? We read of one that "the arms of his hands were made strong by the hands of the mighty God of Jacob." "And that Thine hand might be with me." Mr. Hart in that wonderful hymn of his, "What it is to be a Christian," speaks like this in one verse,

"Every moment be receiving
Strength, and yet be always weak."

Now that exactly describes the way the Lord deals with His people. They receive strength, sufficient strength continually, and yet never loose their sense of weakness, their sense of absolute dependence upon the power of God. "And that Thine hand might be with me." How are temptations to be overcome? How is sin to be resisted and the devil vanquished? Not in our own strength certainly, but only by the hand of God upon us. And it is he who gives power: "Not by might, nor by power, but by My Spirit, saith the Lord of

Hosts." Jabez could only hope to overcome his enemies as the hand of God was with him. See how he felt his dependence.

Then he says, "And that Thou wouldest keep me from evil that it may not grieve me." What a suitable prayer this is, "that Thou wouldest keep me from evil." Do you not find your hearts, some of you, ever prone to run into evil? Mr. Hart confesses,

> "That mariner's mad part I played,
> That sees, yet strikes the shelf."

What a great deal of keeping we need, at least I do. I have to prove that I am quite incapable of keeping myself.

> "To do what's right unable quite,
> And almost as unwilling."

"That Thou wouldest keep me from evil." "Kept," says Peter, "by the power of God through faith unto salvation ready to be revealed in the last time." "And that Thou wouldest keep me from evil, that it may not grieve me." You see, if a child of God is entangled in any evil thing, it is sure to bring him a crop of trouble. If he transgresses, if he oversteps the bounds in any particular, there is sure to be a rod in pickle for him, for, "Whom the Lord loveth He chasteneth, and scourgeth every son whom He receiveth." "And that Thine hand might be with me, and that Thou wouldest keep me from evil;" and only God can, and He is

> "So strong to deliver, so good to redeem,
> The weakest believer that hangs upon Him."

"Keep me from evil;" evil of all sorts, evil within me, evil without me; for

> "All things to promote our fall,
> Show a mighty fitness."

"Keep me from evil that it may not grieve me."

"And God granted him that which he requested." As I said almost at the outset, he called on the God of Israel, the God who hears prayer, the God who does things for those who trust in Him, "And God granted him that which he requested." O if it is in your heart to pray this prayer of Jabez unto the God of Israel, He will not be a barren wilderness to you; and indeed, He is able to do exceeding abundantly above all that we ask or think. He gives beyond the asking. What a mercy that He does, because after all, in our best petitions we are very contracted, our askings are very limited: unbelief has a great hand in limiting our petitions, but the Lord is able to do exceedingly abundantly above all we can ask or think. We little realise what great things a praying soul is warranted to ask at the throne of grace. "Open thy mouth wide," says the Lord, "and I will fill it." We open our mouths so little in our petitions, do we not? I have repeated before now, the words of one of the old Scotch divines, who said, "Seek a little grace from the Lord because you deserve no more? You do not deserve even that, therefore seek a whole sea of grace of Him. Seek not according as your worthiness warrants you to seek, but ask as it becomes His grace and His glory to give." O may the Lord enlarge our hearts to bring large petitions to His mercy seat, to ask great things of Him, yea, to be satisfied with nothing short of Himself; because after all, to be blessed indeed is to be blessed with the Lord God for our God; to have Him say to us, "I am thy God, I am thy Redeemer, thy Husband, thy Surety, thy Friend, thy Strong Tower, thy All in All."

"Less than Thyself will not suffice
My comfort to restore,
More than Thyself I cannot crave,
And Thou canst give no more,"

"O that Thou wouldest bless me indeed;"

"Thyself bestow, for Thee alone,
My all in all, I pray."

May then this prayer of Jabez be written upon our hearts, and the substance of it be breathed out at the mercy seat again and again. Amen.

REV. CHARLES CLAYTON M.A.

R ev. Charles Clayton M.A. was minister of Trinity Parish,
Cambridge. He was Honorary Canon of Ripon, Rector and
Rural Dean of Stanhope and formerly Senior Fellow and
Tutor of Caius College.

A keen supporter of the Cambridge Prayer Union, he preached to
the students of the University and Theological Halls and Colleges.

His great desire was to help younger men in the ministry by pub-
lishing his sermons and this resulted in the writing of five books in
which he expounded the Scriptures as the word of God and exalted
the Saviour as the Way, the Truth and the Life.

This sermon on the prayer of Jabez is taken from *'Cambridge
Sermons; First Series'*.

Chapter Six

AN URGENT REQUEST GRANTED

෭

"And God granted him that which he requested."
1 Chron. iv. 10.

෭

In writing to Timothy St. Paul informs us that "all Scripture" is given by inspiration of God. He adds likewise that all Scripture is "profitable." Some portions of Scripture however appear to be more profitable and more adapted to edification than others. These portions are therefore worthy of more repeated and devout study. Yet in some chapters, where we should least of all expect to find either doctrine or precept, we suddenly come upon the most comforting and refreshing truths, like a thirsty traveller unexpectedly falling in with a pure stream in a sandy desert.

Such is the case with the passage concerning Jabez from which the text is taken. It occurs among the genealogies of the twelve tribes of Israel; and these genealogical accounts, however useful in their day to the ancient Jews, or however important now to the careful student in theology, might be supposed to possess but little interest for the general reader. The passage, therefore, occurring in the midst of details, to us so abstruse, like a fragrant rose surrounded by thorns, appears to be intended as a recompense for the attentive reader of

God's word; as though it said, "Beware how you neglect any portion
of the inspired records, lest, by doing, you rob your soul of some
exceeding great and precious promise." The whole account is as
follows:-

"And Jabez was more honourable than his brethren: and his
mother called his name Jabez, saying, Because I bare him with
sorrow. And Jabez called on the God of Israel, saying, Oh that Thou
wouldest bless me indeed, and enlarge my coast, and that Thine hand
might be with me, and that Thou wouldest keep me from evil, that it
may not grieve me! And God granted him that which he requested."

These words, in reference to Jabez, will lead me to notice four
different subjects; and may God the Holy Ghost make the exposition
profitable to all our souls!

Let us consider:-

1. His name.

His name was Jabez. "His mother called his name Jabez," i.e.,
Sorrowful, "because she bare him with sorrow." "Children and the
fruit of the womb, are an heritage and gift that cometh of the Lord."
But, like other gifts of God, they are not unmixed with trouble.
Through the sin of Eve, all children are born into the world with
sorrow. The sentence upon woman, ever since the fall, is "In sorrow
shalt thou bring forth children." Some mothers have more sorrow
than others; and in many cases the man-child's birth is the mother's
death. It may be that the mother of Jabez might have died in
childbirth; and that, just before she departed, she gave him the name
he afterwards bore, to perpetuate the remembrance of her fatal sorrow.
It was thus that Rachel, the wife of Jacob, acted. As she died, she
called her newly-born child, "Benoni," the son of my grief; but Jacob,
who did not approve of that title, called him "Benjamin," the son of
the right hand. It was thus, too, the wife of Phineas acted, under
similar circumstances. When she heard that the ark of the Lord was
taken, and that her father-in-law Eli as well as her own husband
were dead, she heed not the congratulations of the women who stood

by her, and who said, "Fear not, for thou hast borne a son." She answered them not, nor regarded, but named the child "Ichabod," "where is the glory?" "the glory is departed;" and then she bowed her head and gave up the ghost, in the bitterness of her soul.

It may be however that Jabez's mother survived his birth, and that she gave him this name for other purposes. She gave him the name that it might be a memorandum to herself, to be thankful to God for bringing her through this her sorrow, and to look ever to Him for future deliverances. Every time she called her son by name, she would be reminded of her past mercies, even as Samuel was reminded by the stone he raised at Ebenezer; and she would feel assured thereby that the Lord her God would be her help in every other needful time of trouble. Now this, brethren, should ever be our object in such memorials. We are all of us more apt to talk of our troubles than our mercies. Yet we ought to wonder, when we think of our sins, that our mercies are so many, and that our troubles are so few. And when we do think of those troubles, we should reflect with thankfulness upon the kindness of that loving Saviour who delivered us out of our past distresses, and who yet doth deliver and who yet will deliver. Or, perhaps, in giving her son this name she wished him ever to bear in mind after life, that "man that is born of woman is of few days and full of misery." She was also anxious to remind her son to love, honour, and cherish his earthly parent, and in everything to be a comfort to her, who had brought him into the world with so much pain to herself. On this Mr. Scott judiciously remarks: "Children should remember how much their parents, especially their mothers, suffered for them, before they became capable of reflection; and they should endeavour by every means to requite them by their kindness and their good conduct. But," he adds "it is basely ungrateful (though alas! very common) for children willingly to cause their mothers still more exquisite and durable anguish by their ill behaviour." May the Holy Spirit, my dear younger hearers, impress these salutary suggestions on all your minds! May he teach you to remember the peculiar blessing attached to filial piety. The fifth commandment, you remember, is the first commandment with "promise."

But whatever might have been the object of his mother in giving her son the name of Jabez, she must have felt abundantly recompensed, if she was now alive; and this is our second subject concerning Jabez.

2. His character.

His mother called her son Jabez-sorrowful: but her sorrow must have "been turned into joy," to see how excellent and eminent a man her son had proved. "A wise son maketh a glad father; whereas a foolish son is a grief to his father and a bitterness to her that bare him." The godly mother will be thankful to se her children settled well in life, and choosing for their partners those only that fear the Lord; but her greatest comfort will be to know that her children's souls are really converted to God by the Holy Spirit. As says St. John, the pious mother knows of no greater joy than to see her children "walk in the truth." This joy must have lightened the heart of the mother of Jabez, if she still survived; for of her son the record is,-"Jabez was more honourable than his brethren." Why this title "honourable" was given to Jabez is not stated. It is given to various persons in the Scriptures. Naaman the Syrian is spoken of as "honourable." This was because he had been successful in war. Certain women are spoken of in the Acts of the Apostles as "honourable." This was because they belonged to the upper ranks of the society. The Bereans are spoken of as being "honourable." This was because they searched the Scriptures daily. Jabez was "honourable," probably on all these accounts. But then the chief reason why he was honourable was evidently because of his personal piety. There is no honour like that "honour which cometh from God only." And He has said, "Them that honour Me I will honour." See how honourable the Lord made Joseph! Whatever he did, the Lord made it to prosper; and wherever he was, whether in Potiphar's house, or in Pharaoh's prison, or in the Egyptian court, the Lord gave him favour amongst all to whom he came. The same was the case with Daniel and with others. They were made "more honourable than their brethren," because of their piety. So it is now also. The pious servant, the pious child, the pious parent, the pious citizen, the pious statesman,- oh! How much more trusted and honoured are they than all others! May you, my brethren, be in this manner "honourable!" May you be marked out among your fellows "as the lily among the thorns," "as the apple tree among the trees of the wood!" It will hereafter matter but little who were your progenitors, or when it was you lived, if you are reckoned "honourable" by your piety. We are not told who Jabez father was, nor what was the age in which he flourished. But God knew his character, and approved it, and that was sufficient. May our names, brethren, if not written in the genealogies of earth, be written in the records of heaven, in the book of life! And then we shall be "honourable" indeed.

But we may leave the name and general character of Jabez, and consider the details of his piety. We now therefore notice:-

3. His request.

We are not told when he offered this petition. He made it probably, like Solomon's prayer for wisdom, when he was setting out in the world. Nothing so much becomes a young man, just launching out into the dangers and temptations and trials of active life, as to acknowledge God in all his ways, and to put himself under the Divine protection and guidance. The same Divine guidance and protection, I would observe, is surely equally needed by the young of the other sex, lest their hearts should be fascinated by the trifles of earth, instead of being fixed on the realities of God's glory in heaven.

Perhaps this was a summary of the prayers which Jabez offered day by day, either alone in secret, or with his family. It is well in our devotional exercises to have some heads or general directions for our guidance. In this way the Lord's Prayer is suggestive of matters to bring before our God; so is our Church Litany, which, as good Mr. Simeon used to observe, supplies a thousand pegs on which to hang ten thousand petitions.

Some think that it was on some particular occasion, when he was straitened or threatened by his enemies, that Jabez offered this petition. If so, he acted wisely by carrying into practice that direction, "Call upon Me in the day of trouble. I will hear thee; and thou shalt glorify Me." Thus did Jacob, when about to meet his brother Esau. And thus did Hezekiah, when commanded to prepare for immediate death. Both received, as did Jabez, an answer of peace. What too, brethren, should be our resolve? Ought it not to be, "What time I am afraid, I will think of and call upon my God"?

And to whom did Jabez pray? It was not to "the gods of the Gentiles." And this may be one cause of why he is spoken of as being so much more honourable than his brethren. They may have become idolaters, while he continued to worship and to supplicate the only true God. He called, it is said, on "the God of Israel," that God who alone heareth and answereth prayer. He was thus a true son of Jacob, who wrestled in prayer with Christ, and who would not let Him go without a blessing, and who was surnamed by the name of Israel, because as a prince he had power with God and prevailed.

How Jabez imitated the example of Jacob is seen from the subject-matter of his petition. The first clause is, "O that Thou wouldest bless me indeed." Or, as the margin has it, "If Thou wilt bless me indeed." In that latter case, it was a vow, and a sense of imperfection; but it may be easily filled up, as from Jacob's vow, "*Then shalt Thou be my God.*" He makes no promise. He leaves that to be understood. To use the illustration of Mr. Henry, he gives to God, as it were, a blank paper, and lets Him write what He thought best; as though he had said, "Lord, if Thou wilt bless me indeed, do with me what Thou wilt; I will be at Thy disposal, and at Thy command for ever." The expression of that prayer is remarkable, that God would "bless me indeed," that "blessing Thou wilt bless me." He thought probably of the promise made to his forefather, Abraham, "In blessing I will bless thee, and thy seed after thee." Divine blessings are real blessings, "blessings indeed." "The blessing of the Lord," says Solomon, "it maketh rich and addeth no sorrow with it."

And here we see the difference between men and God. Men may wish one another a blessing. God only can bestow one. A mother may bless her child; a king may bless his subjects; a minister may bless his people; but they cannot impart a blessing. They can only wish one. But of God it is said, "there the Lord commanded His blessing." "The Lord will command His loving-kindness." "Thou art my king, O God, command deliverances for Jacob." To whom then, brethren, should we seek for success, except to Him, of whom we may say truly, as Balak said of Balaam unwittingly, "I wot that he whom thou cursest is cursed, and he whom thou blessest is blessed,"-blessed indeed?

Jabez's prayer was that "the Lord would enlarge his coast." He seemed to be unable at first to obtain that portion of the land which was assigned to him by the lot. It was still occupied by the Canaanites, whom he could not drive out; and in this prayer he shows that, while he was prepared to use every human means, he felt that it was not his own sword or bow that would prevail for the acquiring of the territory he claimed. He looked to the blessing of the Almighty upon his efforts.

"Do Thou enlarge my coast." It may be brethren, that your worldly circumstances are so straitened, that you oftentimes ask God to enlarge your coast, to provide greater means for your increasing wants; and so to prosper your daily toils, that you may not only be able to provide for your own necessities, and those of your families and dependants, but also may have it in your power "to give" in charity "to him that needeth." In such prayers there is nothing wrong, provided you always ask in submission to God's wisdom, and say, "Nevertheless not as I will, but as Thou wilt." But with respect to enlarging your coast in spiritual matters, you cannot be too importunate. "He giveth more grace." There are lengths and breadths of land still to be occupied by you. These are at present tenanted by your spiritual foes, your evil lusts. These you may ask power to cast out, that all the land may be yours, that you may serve God without distraction; and to this end you may use as your own the next clause of Jabez's prayer, which is, "That Thine hand may be with me." Jabez belonged to the tribe of Judah. In reference to that tribe Moses had prayed, "That their own hands might be sufficient for them!" But Jabez felt that their own hands would be insufficient, altogether helpless, unless God's hand also was joined unto theirs. And what, brethren, can any of you want more than this? To have God's hand with you, leading you, strengthening you, and protecting you against every enemy and assailant?

And this is the last clause of the prayer,-"That Thou wouldest keep me from evil, that it may not grieve me." Jabez here plays upon his own name. He wished to be preserved from evil, that it might not grieve him, that it might not make him a Jabez indeed, a man of sorrow.

And what, brethren, can fill your hearts with sorrow except sin? Was it not this which made David exclaim, "Hide Thy face from my sins, and blot out all mine iniquities?" Was it not this that made Peter go out and weep bitterly? And is it not sin that makes you all so miserable and grieve your souls? Your refuge then is prayer. You must ask the Lord Jesus, not only to "bless you indeed," not only "to enlarge your coast," not only to let "His hand be with you," but also "to keep you from evil," not so much from the evil of suffering, as from the evil of sinning. And will that petition be granted? Yes;-for this is Christ's office. He is called Jesus for this very purpose,-"He shall save His people from their sins." That prayer, "lead us not into temptation, but deliver us from evil," is sure to be answered. It was answered in Jabez's case. This we shall see, while we now notice briefly the forth part of our subject. You have observed Jabez's name, his character, and his request. Now notice:

4. His blessing.

Jabez made a large request. But it was not too large. The record is, "And God granted him that which he requested." All the temporal mercies Jabez had asked, the Lord gave. He blessed Jabez "indeed." He enabled Jabez to cast out the Canaanites; and so to enlarge his coasts. His hand was with Jabez, preserving him from evil, and from every adversary. Jabez accordingly became honourable and prosperous in Israel. And it would seem, by his being mentioned so abruptly here, that his name was well known, when Ezra the scribe wrote these two books of Chronicles. The Jews think that Jabez was eminent for his learning, as well as for his success in war and rank in society, and that he became an eminent doctor or teacher, and left behind him many disciples. This idea is confirmed by the statement (in chap ii.55) that "The families of the scribes dwelt in Jabez," a city which, it is likely, took its name from that excellent man whose character and prayer we are now considering.

But whether these things be so or not, Jabez, no doubt, in those petitions thought at the same time of mercies regarding his soul. Ancient believers saw in the land of Canaan a type of heaven. The wars, in which they were compelled to engage, reminded them of their conflict with their spiritual enemies. Every clause therefore of this prayer was most probably offered in reference to blessings far higher and far more noble. In that view of the subject too, God granted Jabez all that he requested. He enabled Jabez to war a good warfare against the world, the flesh, and the devil. He enlarged his coast, in his soul's experience, so that He saw more and more of the Divine mercy and love towards Him in Christ his Saviour. The Lord preserved Jabez from his great enemy, the devil, and at last gave him inheritance amongst those that are sanctified, in a better and more peaceful world.

And what the Lord did for Jabez, brethren, is He not equally prepared to do for ourselves? Was God ready of old to hear prayer; and is His ear heavy now that it cannot hear? Is His arms shortened that he cannot save? Has He not heard all the petitions you have offered in the name of Jesus? You may think you have asked great things; but you cannot open your mouth too widely, in believing prayer. God is willing to do exceedingly abundantly above all that we can ask or even think. He is willing to bless you in your basket and in your store, and to make all things work together for your good. I do not say that He will always answer your petitions as to temporal things; for we very often ask and wish for that which, if given, would only do us injury. You that are parents exercise a wise discretion as to what your children request of you. And God dealeth with you in such matters as a kind father acts towards the children of his love. But as to spiritual mercies, you may ask with all confidence. You may ask for more deep humility; for a heart-felt contrition for sin; for a clear faith in Christ; for a larger measure of Christian love;

for a greater spirituality of affections; for greater holiness; for greater comfort; for greater usefulness; and for all the gifts and graces of the Holy Spirit. These precious blessings you cannot ask too fervently; and, if you ask them aright, in the name and for the merits of Christ, and with a veiw to devote yourself more and more unreservedly to His service, you may rest assured that you shall have the petitions that you desired of Him; and it shall be said of you, as it was said of Jabez, "And God granted" you, and not only granted you, but also exceeded, "that which you requested."

Such, brethren, are a few lessons furnished by the account here given of Jabez,-

1. *His name.*
2. *His character.*
3. *His request.*
4. *His blessing.*

We hence may derive, in conclusion,-

A sure test of our own state before God.

Are we sorry for sin? What is our name? Is it Jabez? That is sorrowful. Or is it *Isaac*? That is laughter. There is a time to weep and a time to laugh. If we are believers in Christ, we may with good reason be Isaacs, and have our mouths filled with laughter, and our tongues with singing, when we remember what great things the Lord Jesus has done for us, in plucking us as brands out of the everlasting burning.

At the same time we should also bear the name of Jabez. Jabez prayed to be kept from the "evil" of sin, that it might not "grieve" him. If we, too, are believers, we shall feel grief and sorrow by reason of our guilt. The remembrance of our sins will be grievous unto us. The burden of them will be intolerable. We shall weep because of our many shortcomings. We shall have considerable heaviness, by reason of our multiplied transgressions against One to whom we owe so much. Is this your case, my dear brethren? Do you know what it is to shed tears of sorrow for your base ingratitude to your Saviour and your God? Can you say, like Job, "mine eye poureth out tears"? Can you add, like Jeremiah, "for these things my eyes are dim"? Can you, like Paul, exclaim, "O wretched man that I am"?

Again, if you do feel this sorrow, I would apply another test to ascertain your state before God. And that is, Is it your desire to grow in grace? Is it your constant petition,-"O that Thou wouldest enlarge my coast"? My dear hearers, there is no standing still in Divine things. In the heavenly race there is ground behind; and there is ground before, are you forgetting that which is behind and are you pressing forward to that which is before? Are you, by the in-working power of the Holy Spirit, adding to your faith virtue, and to your virtue, love, joy, peace? And is it your aim and desire to go on to perfection? Are you mortifying every sin, and are you striving to bring even every thought into captivity to the obedience of Christ? Remember, brethren, this is the only sure proof of your real conversion, an anxious desire to become holy, even as Christ is holy. On this it is well observed by the Reformer, Luther: "For these 1500 years," he says, "there has not been started a more mischievous and pestilential notion, than that God does not demand a perfect fulfilling of all His laws. God," he adds, "never alters His perfect law, though He pardons us when we break it. Observe how," he continues, "God does not pardon those who are asleep, but those who labour, those who fear, those who say with Job, 'I know that Thou wilt not hold me innocent.'" Yes, He pardons only those who seek to subdue the flesh to the Spirit, and who strive to enlarge their coast by simple reliance on the Holy Spirit's power.

Go forward, then, brethren, in your Christian course, and seek, by the Holy Spirit's aid, an increase in faith, hope, and love; and ere long you will take your place among the angels and all the company of heaven; and then it shall be testified of you, as it was of Jabez, "The Lord granted him that which he requested; all came to pass, not one thing failed."

REV. DAVID JAMISON B.A.

The Rev. David Jamison B.A. was the fifth minister of Second Newtownhamilton Presbyterian Church in Ireland. He was ordained on 27th December, 1865 and showing a great interest in education he was made responsible for the building of schools.

His son Charles Ingram Jamison was ordained as his assistant and became his successor when he retired from the ministry on 6th April 1897.

He died 12 years later on 16th October 1909.

These two sermons on the prayer of Jabez are taken from his volume of sermons entitled *'Benedictions'*.

Chapter Seven

HIS FIRST AND CHIEFEST WISH

⌒

And Jabez was more honourable than his brethren; and his mother
called his name Jabez, saying, Because I bare him with sorrow.
And Jabez called on the God of Israel, saying, Oh that Thou
wouldest bless me indeed!
1 Chronicles iv. 9, 10.

⌒

In this prayer of Jabez we have one of which it may, I think, be said,
that it expresses the longing, conscious or unconscious of us all; and
one therefore which is well worthy of our consideration.

First however, let us look a little at the context. The chapter in which
it occurs does not look at first sight a very inviting one; but surely
these two immediate verses do. The record which they contain is
very brief; but it is at the same time both a taking and a telling one.

Driving along a dreary road, you have possibly at some time come
suddenly upon a charming bit of scenery-scenery which charmed
you all the more because of the surprise and the contrast. The top of
a hill or a turn in the road has brought it unexpectedly to view; and
immediately all the weary, dreary, miserable monotone of the past is
forgotten in the delight and the beauty of present.

We have somewhat a similar experience here; for here in what we might almost call a wilderness of unfamiliar, and no doubt to some of us, almost unpronounceable names, we have at this part of the chapter a quick transition of like surprise and pleasure. It would scarcely be an exaggeration to say that there are not two more refreshing or reassuring verses anywhere in all the Bible, than these two in this otherwise dry chapter of this book of Chronicles. They formed one of the greenest of oases in one of the most bleak and barren of deserts.

Of the history of Jabez, it is true, we know but little. Indeed with the possible exception of a reference to him in the second chapter, the record here exhaust the whole account we have of him. But, like a telescope, these verses, notwithstanding, discover to us a morning star aglow through all the haze of far remoteness, whose special brightness cheers and gladdens us; or, to alter the metaphor, the portrait here, though but a miniature, depicts to us a kingly, kindly man, who, we are somehow sure, lived well and noble long ago; and who, though dead, yet speaks to us in winning, wholesome, hearty words at once of courage and of comfort, of counsel and of cheer.

Of most, if not of all, whose names the chronicler enumerates in the chapter, we know absolutely nothing save their names; but Jabez himself is an illustrious illustration that the righteous shall be held in everlasting rememberance. In his prayer also, which is here recorded, we have evidently indicated the keynote of his character; the polestar of his life. And when we read it, we wonder no longer that Ezra, or the author whoever he may have been, perhaps compiler rather, of these books of Chronicles, should, when he came to this name in the genealogical researches, and memory flashed upon it the halo of this remembered prayer, have paused for a while from his more prosaic work to record it here,

Such a prayer deserved to live. The Bible, we might almost say, had been a poorer book without it. Of all its many gems this is not the least bright or brilliant. Among all its many worthies Jabez holds by no means the least important place. Passing as is the glance we get of him, he fastens himself upon our notice immediately, irresistibly, and fascinates at once our approval and our affection.

Though, so to speak, we see him but a moment, as he comes abreast of us in the long procession, the momentary encounter yet monuments him in our memories as one of nature's true nobility; and it gives us at the same time, if we be at all impressionable, a felt and forcible momentum to follow his ennobling example.

The tenth verse of the chapter here, may we not say, fully explains and endorses the ninth. We have 'Honourables' now, and 'Right Honourables,' so styled; and often apart from place or pedigree or office or property, it is difficult to discover the fitness of the distinction in some of the cases at least. But Jabez was an 'Honourable' indeed, one of God's 'Honourables;' and we cannot as we read this prayer, be unwilling to allow the applicability of the title to him, since he manifests unmistakably the genuine aristocracy intimated by our Laureate in well-worn words,

> Howe'er it be, it seems to me
> 'Tis only noble to be good:
> Kind hearts are more than coronets,
> And simple faith than Norman blood.

There is evidently no vulgar pride about the man who prays as Jabez does; no supercilious presuming, no overweening confidence in self. A thoughtful, prayerful, resolute man, whose goal is duty, and whose fear is sin; whose affection and whose ambition, rectitude; and his defence and dependence, prayer; Jabez here is beckoning all of us to a higher level of life than that which the many are too content to tread: and we are assured at the same time by his biography, brief though it is, that God is ever true to His promise-"Them that honour Me I will honour;" and that if not always uniform, the experience at all events is always universal-"Godliness is profitable unto all things, having promise to the life that now is, and of that which is to come."

His life indeed began in the shadow of some sore grief; for his name signifies the 'sorrowful,' and his mother gave it him "because" as she tells us, "I bare him with sorrow." But ere long we are sure, as we read his prayer, the clouds dispersed; and his subsequent life, all the purer and fresher because of them, like the clearer shining after rain, if she were spared to see it, dried his mother's tears for the past, or it may be dismissed her fears for the future; and gave to her melancholy prognostic a complete and winsome, and we may be certain, a welcome refutation. Her sorrow we cannot doubt, when we turn to the concluding clause of the story, was soon turned into joy; the water of her spirit of heaviness transmuted by the miracle-working of prayer into the wine of abounding thankfulness.

It maybe that she lived at a time when the nation was subdued in tributary, she mourned in patriotic piety over its fallen fortunes; or grieved in godly sorrow over its broken vows; or perhaps her grief, more personal in its cause, was owing to the fretting memory of higher rank or of greater wealth which once her family possessed; or it maybe, since no father's name is given here, that she had lost her husband ere her boy was born, or that at his birth she had more than ordinary experience of woman's painful reminder of the Fall: or, possibly, there may be truth in the conjecture, which places Jabez in history as a relative and contemporary of Achan, whose sorrowful story we read in the book of Joshua; and that it was the recent judicial stoning of him and his, because of the wedge of gold and the Babylonish garment, that overshadowed his mother's spirit at the time of his birth, and prompted her to this projection of the shadow into the name of her child.

However this may be, the name at all events became very speedily a misnomer; though even so we cannot altogether account it a mistake. In the history of Jabez, briefly as it is told, we have a hint that the very meaning of his name exercised a healthful influence upon his character; and by its remembered significance forewarned him and forearmed to its disproof. In the latter part of his prayer, obscured somewhat in our translation, there is a reference to the meaning of his name which makes this probable, for when he prays, 'Keep me from evil, that it may not *grieve* me!' he uses the verbal form of the noun which composes his name, and prays in effect, that thought sorrowful in name, he may not be sorrowful in fact and experience, he says 'I am called the sorrowful, but let not evil in its mastery over me, in its effects upon me, make me the sorrowful indeed.'

"As his name is, so is he; Nabal (Fool) is his name, and folly is with him," said Abigail as she pleaded with David for the life of her husband. Jabez here makes a like allusion to the meaning of his name, and prays that as it was so he might not be. Does he not indicate too, as he does so, the true 'genesis' of sorrow; and may we not farther say that he indicates also the true 'exodus' of escape and deliverance from it? For, may not sorrow be truthfully described as the shadow, which is cast and caused by sin; and do we not then get away from the gloom and into the sunshine only in the proportion in which we "cease to do evil and learn to do well?"

But now, let us look at the prayer rather than any longer, interesting though he is, at the pray-er.

It is in every respect a model; and we would all of us do well to make it in its entirety our own. Especially those of us who are just starting in life, or who are on the brink of some critical or important undertaking; but indeed all of us, if only we have begun to face the realities of our position and our prospects-we could not do better than follow the example of Jabez here.

This indeed is the royal road, the king's highway to honour; to credit; to respectability; to comfort; to assured advance and solid success in life. This will fit us for life's duties; arm us against life's dangers; acquaint us with life's true consolations; lift us to life's real dignities. This will make life in its progress a happy stepping heavenwards; and life at its close a peaceful, hopeful, joyful, retrospect-this, that is to say, humble and earnest enlistment of God as our guardian and guide; this casting ourselves on Him as "Our shield and our exceeding great reward;" this acknowledging Him in all our ways that He may direct our steps.

They make a very grave and great mistake, let us all be assured, even in connection with our life and experiences on earth who pray, as only too many do practically pray to God, saying-"Depart from us, for we desire not the knowledge of thy ways:" for a life without God is and must be ever a life without happiness; a life without hope in the world: while on the other hand, all experience endorses the counsel of Scripture- "Acquaint now thyself with Him and be at peace: thereby good shall come to thee:" and proves the truth of its distinct declaration-"Behold, the righteous shall be recompensed in the earth: much more the wicked and the sinner."

Jabez, we are here told first, "Called upon the God of Israel." No doubt he was surrounded by idolaters; and by this statement is simply by the historian here differenced from them. He recognised God as the one only and true God; and so, as matter of course, addressed his prayer to Him alone. We need not, perhaps, to have his example dwelt upon in this respect, since from idolatry, in its grosser forms at least, we are happily remote. But in another respect perhaps we do: for do we really call upon the God of Israel; and do we all and always do it with the evident expectancy, and with the habitual usualness with which it would seem Jabez did it?

Do we, in other words, recognise God, as in very truth "the Giver of every good and perfect gift;" a "God nigh to us in all things that we call upon Him for?" Do we bring to Him our every concern; consult Him in our every experience; lay before Him our every want and wish; defer to Him and depend upon Him at all times and for all things? Or, do we practically act and think as if while we needed God at some time and for some things, yet at other times and for other things we can do without Him?

Are we, in fine, and indeed "careful for nothing, but in all things by prayer and supplication to make known our request unto Him with thanksgiving."

If so we have learned a secret which is a sovereign specific against the frets and worries which rob the lives of many men of much sunshine; and which robe them instead in needless depression and anxiousness and gloom. But if not, we have a great deal yet to learn not merely as to the real comfort of life, but as to its right conduct as well.

Everything, let us at length realize if we have not, that is a matter of care to us, we may make and we ought to make a matter of prayer to God. "All our need" is the only limit He imposes; and He has promised to supply all our need "according to His riches in glory, by Christ Jesus." The God of Israel therefore is one Who cares for all the interests of all His people; and in connection with no part or department of their lives whatever shall they come short of any true blessing, or any real benefit who seek their all from Him. Of this we may abundantly certify ourselves, for surely the Psalmist is right in singing:

> For God the Lord's a sun and shield,
> He'll grace and glory give;
> And will withhold *no good* from them
> That uprightly do live.

And equally surely the logic of Paul is irresistible when he asks in Romans 8th chapter-"He that spared not His own Son, but delivered Him up for us all, how shall He not with Him also freely give us all things!"

To proceed however, Jabez as he calls upon the God of Israel begins his prayer with the wishful, wistful utterance-"Oh that thou wouldest bless me indeed." And confining our attention to it at present, let me ask you to notice first, in connection with this petition,

ITS DIRECTNESS.

Jabez, it is evident here, was really conscious of want, and really anxious for supply. He was confident too that God could supply, and therefore he applies and appeals to Him that He would. He tells out his want simply, and he urges it upon God strongly. Many prayers are simply a roundabout stringing together of empty sentences without point and without purpose; born of no desire and aimed at no outcome. It was not so with Jabez. He "directed his prayer unto God and looked up." His expressed words were embodied wishes; and he speaks them out without circumlocution and without verbiage. His, too, was no run-away knock at the door of mercy; but a knock that the door might be opened. It was no mere complimentary address to God; but an address that sought from God the complement of acceptance and of answer. He prays in the hope and with the object that God will hear and grant his prayer: he knows what he says, and means what he says; he knows to Whom he addresses, and so he expects and waits to be answered.

Should we not copy Jabez in this! Let us learn if we have not, to pray as he did-really conscious of want, and really concerned about supply. "The body," our Lord tells us, "is more than raiment," and similarly we may say that what is wanted in prayer is not fineness of dress, but realness of address; not vain repetitions, but very petitions; not much speaking, but much seeking; nature, not art; feeling, not phrase; fact, not form. In a word, to paraphrase the language of Paul where he tells us who the true Jew is, 'That is not a prayer that is one outwardly, neither is that praying which is outward from the lips; but that is a prayer that is one inwardly, and praying is that of the heart, in the spirit and not in the letter, whose praise is not of men but of God."

But farther, a second thing which strikes us in this prayer of Jabez is,

ITS EARNESTNESS.

His praying is very real and very forceful. In the first chapter of James' epistle, where that the apostles speak of Elias as praying 'fervently,' the margin of our Bibles give us the alternative reading, "Elias prayed in his prayer." So also did Jabez here. He really looked upon God, and looked up to God as the Hearer of prayer; he came to Him believing that He is, and that He is the rewarder of them that fear Him; and his petition was the outcome of felt necessity, the out pouring of fervent desire.

And this, need it be said, is the true way to pray? How many of us do so? How many of us "pray in our prayers?" Praying in our prayers is praying in deed and in truth. Merely to 'say our prayers,' if not at its worst a mockery, is yet at its best an unreality and a snare. Let us all cultivate a true spirit of prayer and of supplication! Let our prayers be the offering up of our desires, the pouring out of our hearts; then we shall appreciate its privileges and experience its power. To pray as Jabez did, will ever be to be heard and to be helped as Jabez was: for where the praying is actual, there it is effectual also. Here let it also be said in passing, that while "oh thats" and "indeeds" are not perhaps very elegant forms of expression, nor would their repetition please the fastidious, yet they are nevertheless good words in prayer, if only the earnestness which they express is real; and more, we also may say for them, that this earnestness if real is also itself an *earnest-*an earnest of answer, and of answer, too, exceeding abundant above all we know to ask or think. God's wont with all his people is to do as He did for example with Solomon. See 1 Kings, chapter iii, and read from the 5th to the 15th verse.

But again, a third noticeable feature here in the petition of Jabez is,

ITS DISCRIMINATION.

All is not gold that glitters: and all is not blessing that seems to be so. Blessing is, indeed, a relative word. What would be a blessing to one man might be the very reverse of a blessing to another. Nay, in the case even of the same person, what at one time would be a benefit and a help, might at another time prove instead a bane and hindrance.

Jabez manifests here his wisdom in this, that while he had, no doubt, his own predilections and preferences, his own opinions of what would be for his good; he yet holds and desires these only in subservience to the higher will and in deference to the greater wisdom of God: and we may understand him as praying in effect, as he utters the words we are considering-"Oh that Thou wouldest give me"-not that which seems to me or to those about me a blessing; but wouldest give me that which Thou knowest shall prove in my experience to be-"a blessing indeed." If even it should be disappointment of cherished expectations, delay of kindled hopes, defeat of life-long purposes; if even it should be trial, mortification, disaster, apparent discomfiture, failure to the eye of flesh-no matter, if only Thou bless me indeed. Jabez, in other words, if we read his prayer aright, may be taken as distrusting himself, and casting himself with the fullest confidence upon the love and wisdom, the goodness and judgement of God.

Here again, then, is he not a model we all should imitate? For while, and especially perhaps in connection with earthly things, we should ever honestly and humbly state in prayer our own real wishes and real conceptions of what would be good for us; should we not also guard ourselves against very possible mistakes-very possible misunderstandings of selves, and miscalculation of sequence, by the adoption in all doubtful matters of such a proviso as that which even the Lord Himself employed, when praying in Gethsemane, He said ere He closed- "Nevertheless, not as I will, but as Thou wilt."

We are but children of a larger growth; and we know what is best for us: should we not therefore confide ourselves with more abandon and with greater confidence to the care and wisdom of Him who knows us thoroughly everyone; Who sees the end from the beginning, and of Whom, too, we read elsewhere in these books of Chronicles, that "The eye of the Lord run to and fro throughout the whole earth, to show Himself strong in the behalf of them whose heart is perfect (*i.e.* sincerely) towards Him"-of Whom too we have the kindred assurance in the New Testament scriptures, oft quoted but not always realised in feeling-though always realised in fact-that "all things shall work together for good to those which love God, and to those who are the called according to His purpose."

The things which we would think would be for us, might prove instead to be really and sadly against us. While, on the other hand, at the very times and connection with the very things of which, Jacob-like, we are inclined to say-"All these things are against me," we may live to see as he did that what we feared were converging links in an iron chain of evil destiny, were instead the conveying links in a golden chain of out coming and oncoming blessing. Let us always remember in praying that things agreeable to God's will must necessarily and certainly, if we only trust Him, be things advantageous to our welfare; while things on the other hand agreeable to our own will might not be so, might be very far from being so. And thus let us ever intreat of God, as we may interpret Jabez here, that if at any time, or in respect to anything, we in our folly or ignorance should "ask amiss," He would yet of His grace and in His wisdom answer aright.

But once more and lastly in connection with this first portion of the prayer of Jabez, we shall not be wrong, if as read for our employment now, we recognise in it a reference to higher than merely earthly blessings-a reference in fact to those blessings which we all should especially desire-the blessing which have to do, not so much with the outer as with the inner self; not so much with the body as with the soul-the blessings, in a word, which are described in the New Testament as "all spiritual blessings in heavenly places in Christ Jesus."

For us indeed, however it may have been with Jabez-for us who have now the advantage of a higher discovery and development of truth and of teaching than Jabez had, this is the especial meaning of this earnest utterance.

Spiritual blessings are the main wants of our nature, the main constituents of our happiness, and these therefore we should chiefly desire. They constitute our main endowment for the experiences of the present; our chief equipment for the expectancies of the future. And to have these-to have, for example, the blessing of the man whose iniquity is pardoned, and whose sin is covered; to have the blessing which is better and higher than the blessing of only pardon, the blessing of being "turned away from our iniquities;" to have first, the blessing of such a true conviction of our sinfulness as shall rouse us in earnest to the question-"What shall I do to be saved?" to have the blessing then of such a real apprehension of the mercy of God in Christ as shall attract us to Him and bring us to receive and rest upon Him for our salvation; then, after this, to have the blessing of such a conscious sense of obligation to Christ as shall lift us by the leverage of love to a higher and purer and nobler level of life; to have the blessing along with this, of such an indwelling and inworking of the Holy Spirit in our spirits as shall both dispose and enable us to die indeed unto sin and live unto righteousness; and yet in addition to all, to have the blessing of being guided by the counsel and kept by the power of God; to have the blessing, in fine, of a living and working faith, of a lifting and labouring love, of a preserving and purifying hope: or, to put it shorter still, to have the blessing of a real return and a right relation to God, through an humble and earnest trust in Jesus Christ our Lord-to have blessings like these is really to be "blessed indeed;" and only in the proportion in which we have these can we be properly said to be indeed blessed.

For to have these, is to be leaving the night and the blight of sin and its consequences behind us, and to be experiencing the light of that morning dawn which shineth more and more unto the perfect day. To have these, is to have blessings which brighten and last; and to have blessings too, which not merely endure but enhance and enlarge, until, at length, they mount into and merge in the perfect blessedness of an unalloyed, an unshadowed and an unending Heaven.

Indeed other blessings without these-*i.e.*, without spiritual blessing-are scarcely blessings at all, for while what men speak of as the blessing of this life and are good enough ingredients in the cup of human experience, they need the milk and meat of Gospel Sustenance, and the oil and wine of Gospel Cure and Cheer, to make them really solacing or satisfying to the soul-the soul which, without these latter, better things, must ever cry, and cry in vain, "O, who will show us any good." The "nether springs" have their uses and their values; but the blessings of the "upper springs" are incomparably the best. Let these then be our chief desire. Like Paul, let us count all things but loss for the excellency of the knowledge which is in Christ Jesus: like Mary, choose the good part that can never be taken from us: let us "covet earnestly the best gifts:" let us "seek first the kingdom of God and His righteousness!"

The very brightest and best of the blessings of earth are the veriest vanities, in default of an interest in Christ, so far as any real gain or any solid satisfaction is concerned. A man might have them all in abundance and yet be poor and wretched, and miserable and blind and naked, and of all men most miserable; but if we have Christ first, then "all things are ours, and we are Christ's, and Christ is God's."

Nay, even the reproach of Christ is greater riches than all the treasures of Egypt; and it is better-infinitely better if the will of God be so-to suffer affliction with the people of God, than to enjoy any or all of the so-called pleasures of sin. For on the one hand, the pleasures of sin are but for a season-and then there is the wages of sin, which is death; and on the other hand, the light afflictions of the people of God are but for a season too-"but for a moment" the apostle says-and they work out for them a far more exceeding and eternal weight of glory.

To conclude however for the present, is it not true that 'Blessing' is a word which represents that which, whether we call it by this name or by another, we all and always especially desire? Is it not true also that in desiring to be blessed, we all desire to be blessed 'indeed'-to be blessed in actual fact and not in exciting fancy-blessed in solid substance and not merely in shadowy semblance-blessed in real and permanent experience, and not simply and only in ephemeral and passing emotion?

If this be so then, and it is so, let us all carry away this lesson from the record here, that we go the only right way to work in seeking to secure such blessing, when we take the plan of Jabez, and expect it in trustful and earnest desire from the dependence upon Him Who alone can gauge the guerdon and true and real longings of an immortal human soul; and Who, as "the God and Father of our Lord Jesus Christ, and the Father of mercies, and the God of all comfort," invites the application of all, and will never cheat the expectation nor disappoint the experience of any.

Only let us trust Him; only let us be willing to believe, as surely we may and ought, that His notion and method of blessing must be right, however meantime they both may differ from ours; only to, while we remember and acknowledge our own unworthiness of even the least of His mercies-let us stretch out the hand of faith that we may freely receive for Jesus' sake. Then that God Who, to quote Paul's argument again, has already not spared His own son but deliver Him up for us all, will, we may beyond all controversy be certain, with him also freely give us all things-all things, that is to say, suitable and sufficient for us here-all things we need to conduce to earthly, and to conduct eternal blessedness; and then in the great hereafter we shall equally, certainly find-

What no human eye has seen,
What no mortal ear has heard,
What on thought has never been
In its highest flight conferred-

That has God prepared in stone
For his people evermore.

Just one other word. "Oh that Thou wouldest bless me indeed," is a longing God alone can satisfy. Gold cannot; rank cannot; fame cannot; learning cannot; pleasure cannot; mere worldly success, all worldly supply cannot. Nothing, and no one can but God Himself. He, however, both certainly can and will. Forsee, at the end of the 10th verse, how the prayer of Jabez sped: and remember there is no respect of person with God! What he did for Jabez, He is equally willing, equally certain to do for me and for you.

Let us but approach Him, confessing our sins, and praying forgiveness and favour for Jesus' sake. Then taking thus our true attitude, and, so to speak, enabling God to put aside the sword of His challenging Justice by the sceptre of His compassionating Grace, our experience of Him and of greatness of His goodness shall be such, that thereafter we shall sing with a new endorsement, because of our personal discovery, the Psalm to which David's heart was long ago attuned, and which speaks of the comfort and confidence, the grateful uplook and the glad and certain outlook, of every true believer-

O greatly blessed the people are
The joyful sound that know;
In the brightness of Thy face, O Lord,
They ever on shall go.
They in Thy name shall all the day
Rejoice exceedingly,
And in Thy righteousness shall they
Exalted be on high.

And shall we not thankfully add with him-

All blessing to the Lord our God
Let be ascribed then,
For evermore so let it be.
Amen, yea, and Amen.

Chapter Eight

THE REMAINDER OF HIS PRAYER, AND HOW IT SPED

❧

"And Jabez called on the God of Israel, saying, Oh that Thou wouldest bless me indeed, and enlarge my coast, and that thine hand might be with me, and that thou wouldest keep me from evil, that it may not grieve me! And God granted him that which he resquested." 1 Chronicles iv.10.

❧

We have already considered the opening sentence of this bright and brief biography-a little but lovely oasis in a desert of dry genealogical records.

We have also examined the first petition of the comprehensive prayer embalmed in it. We have noticed its directness as a real appeal and application to God-a prayer in fact as well as in form, in feeling as well as in phrase. We have seen its earnestness-an earnestness which should evidently be always a feature in all the prayers of all of us: for surely when we pray we should not merely assume the posture and use the phraseology of prayer, but we should also cherish its spirit; and make its sentence the vehicles of real requests.

We have further remarked its discriminateness, chiefly as manifesting that self-distrust and diffidence which certainly becomes us always in all our approaches and addresses to Him who knows us better than we know ourselves, and in connection with Whom we maybe ever confident that He will do the best thing at the best time and in the best shape and way, for all of those who really trust in Him and call upon Him in sincerity and truth.

We have traced in it, too, for us at least who live in New Testament teaching, a reference to those spiritual blessings which as immortal beings constitute our especial need, contribute our especial benefit, and should therefore occupy our chief affection and anxiety.

Whatever may be our position or property or prospects on earth, we know if we know anything at all, that here we have no abiding portion or continuing city: and we know also that after this world is the next; and that our prospects there hing and hinge upon our preparation here.

Evidently then to be "blessed indeed" is to be blessed with blessing that shall reach and enrich our inward and immortal selves; and not merely touch our outward lot our passing life: blessings that shall not only brighten, that is to say, and beautify our earthly experiences; but which too, instead of shrinking and shrivelling into nothingness at the approach of death, shall then be crowned, completed and consummated by an invitation into the joy of our Lord, and an introduction into "the inheritance incorruptible and undefiled and that fadeth not away."

How sad, how unspeakably sad their position is, however bright their earthly lot, who have nothing before them in the eternal future but "a certain fearful looking for of judgement and of fiery indignation which shall devour the adversaries," and who must say if they realise the truth-"When a few years are come, then I shall go the way whence I shall not return." But how glad, on the other hand, how unspeakably glad is the condition of those, however much it maybe true of them here and now-"Man that is born of woman is of a few days and is full of trouble," who, casting backward its brightness upon all the present, have in the great hereafter "a looking for the blessed hope and the glorious appearing of the great God and our saviour Jesus Christ," and who can say in addition with the Psalmist-

Goodness and mercy all my life
Shall surely follow me;
And in God's house for evermore,
My dwelling place shall be.

This, let us remember, this latter is the heritage at once inestimable and inalienable of every believer in Jesus. Jesus Christ who died for us, who loved us and gave Himself for us, is One who not only says to all his people, "Verily, Verily, I say unto you, whosoever keepeth my saying shall never taste of death;" but He is One also whose pledge and guarantee to each of them is-"Lo, I am with you always even to the end of the world." Not only then may they trust Him fully about their eternal interests and say each one, "I know whom I have believed, and am persuaded He is able to keep that which I have committed to Him;" but they may count with the fullest possible confidence, also, in connection with all their earthly experiences, that He will "supply all their needs." For is not this His own sure word of promise-"Seek ye first the kingdom of God and His righteousness, and all these things (the what to eat and to drink, and the wherewithal to be clothed) shall be added unto you:" and is this not His own authorisation against all anxiety-"Take no thought of the morrow: for the morrow shall take thought for the things of itself?"

But with this, by way of recapitulation, let us now consider the remainder of this prayer of Jabez. The petitions, which follow, are equally worthy of our attention and of our adoption as the first.

It is true that the second-

"AND ENLARGE MY COAST,"

Looks as if its modern counter part would be, 'Increase my property; better my position and prospects in life;' and so it may seem at first sight as if it were entirely of the earth, earthy.

But even if we read it so, it is not out of place or out of keeping with the preceding utterance. The Bible which says, "Seest thou a

man diligent in his business; he shall stand before kings; he shall not stand before mean men," is not a book which discountenances or discourages a temperate or healthy ambition. Nor need anyone fear that within due limits it is wrong for him or for her to harbour the natural desire to lift one's self if it may be, to a higher level of life.

Only let this second petition be *second* to the first and subordinate to it: only let it be after the first and, so to speak, in its shadow, and we need not fear to cherish it nor think that we act amiss in making it a part of our prayer.

Where the fault in this regard comes in is, where men put a petition of this kind first; and where too they seek for earthly prosperity without taking into account its possibly pernicious influence on that which is higher and better; their seeking, that is to say, unmodified and unmoderated by a jealous and prior carefulness about their eternal interests. John wrote to Gaius-"Beloved, I wish above all things that thou mayest prosper and be in health, and even as thy soul prospereth." Did we seek even for great things in this spirit, on this understanding, with this proviso, I do not think the embargo of Jeremiah to Baruch would then apply-"Seek them not."

Let us always seek first God's kingdom and His righteousness; first in time; first in preference; and first in our recognition of their relative importance; and then we may safely seek, seeking in difference to the Divine will and in dependence upon Divine wisdom, even for earthly advantages.

This petition of Jabez, read in the light of the petition which precedes it, is but the prayer of Agur the son of Jakeh-"Two things have I required of thee; deny me not them before I die: Remove far from me vanity and lies: give me neither poverty nor riches; feed me with food convenient for me; lest I be full and deny Thee and say, 'Who is the Lord?' or lest I be poor and steal, and take the name of my God in vain." And it is, moreover, a petition no more out of joint or out of harmony with the other petitions here than is the petition "Give us this day our daily bread" out of line with the other petitions in the model prayer which the Lord Himself taught His disciples.

Men read their Bibles very, very strangely, if they think that prayer about our temporal concerns is either an impertinence or an intrusion in His regard Who would have us "Cast all our cares on Him," and to Whom the earth belongs and the fulness thereof just as much as the heavens do and the treasuries there. On the contrary, the more we consult God and depend upon Him in temporal matters just as we do in spiritual, we do the better; and it shall be the better with and for us. Instead of our sacred things being secularised by the contact and connection, as some seem to fear they would; our secular things shall rather be made sacred. Prosperity sought from God, and if God will, is altogether a different thing from the prosperity which is sought instead of God or without God. May we not, besides adapt a text of Scripture and say, 'The body and the soul meet together; THE LORD is the Maker of them both?"

This petition, however, "And enlarge my coast," is being capable of being interpreted in another way. Jabez, it is probable, lived about the time when the Land of Promise was being or had lately been partitioned amongst the several tribes and families of Israel; and some part of the portion allotted to him was yet, it may be, when he uttered this prayer, in possession of the Canaanites, devoted to destruction. These, therefore it was alike his interest, and his duty, as soon as possible, to dispossess. This he knows to be his duty, recognises to be his interest; and here he is setting about the doing of it; humbly and trustfully, first of all seeking the aid of God that he may do it successfully.

A closer modern counterpart then to this second petition of Jabez - closer in some respects at least - would be this: 'Help me, O Lord, to a larger Christian life - to a life more devoted to duty, more removed from sin, more sanctified in all its parts and phrases. There is still a law in my members warring against the law of my mind: I am conscious still of the presence and power within me of appetites and wishes and passions and feelings and inclinations that are usurpers within my soul: help me, O Lord, to overcome them, to oust them, to purify myself from all filthiness of the flesh and the spirit: forgetting the things that are behind and reaching forth unto the things that are before, help me to press towards the mark for the prize of the high calling in Christ Jesus.'

This we may say is the Old Testament prayer of Jabez put in New Testament language; and so interpreted, it is surely a fitting prayer for every Christian. Past advances should satisfy none: much former evil may have been removed from our lives; and sanctification may have reclaimed already somewhat of our natures, making our heart the home of true dispositions, and our life a land of promise. But much is yet to be removed from every man's heart and habits and life if he would be in every respect what he ought. And as he realises this, and rouses himself, like Jabez here, to fight the good fight of faith, and to conquer back again his whole soul and spirit and body from all the Canaanities of earthliness and sin, is it not his true policy, his proper course, to solicit to his aid, as Jabez did, the power of Him Who alone in such a warfare can "teach his hands to war and his fingers to fight"-without Whom he can indeed do nothing; but having Whom upon his side he can say with Paul, "I can do all things through Christ Who strengtheneth me."

This Jabez does not only in this petition but more particularly perhaps in the next which is intimately connected with it. He there goes on to plead,

"AND THAT THINE HAND MAY BE WITH ME."

Prayer with Jabez, let us here observe, is not a substitute for action but a prelude to it; not an alternative but an ally. While he prays, he also contemplates and counts upon effort.

And this is a lesson from his example, which we too would do well to learn and to learn more thoroughly. These two must be joined if either the prayer is to be heard or the effort to be successful. Prayer without effort is hypocrisy: effort without prayer is presumption: the one way to succeed is to combine the two. Sin shall ever be to many for us if we attack it unaided, however sincere our struggle or earnest our effort: we shall never experience even when best resolved that "the good which we could we do not; and the evil which we would not, that we do." On the other hand also, that prayer is plainly not honest, not real, which does not express itself in application as well as in supplication; in endeavour as well as entreaty.

If we wish, and we ought to do so; if we really wish to be better, and to do better; if we desire our lives to become less marred by inconsistency and more marked by sincerity and loyalty; less conformed to this world and more transformed by the renewing of our minds: if we would be enabled more and more to die unto sin and to live unto righteousness; if we need desire to grow in grace and to grow up unto Him in all things who is our Head, even Christ; then the true way to compass our desires-and the one way to do so, is to pray ever and earnestly to Him who will "work in us to will and to do of His good pleasure;" and at the same time to work ever and earnestly too-working out as God works in-"Working out our own salvation with fear and trembling."

Thus, praying and working, God's hand will be with us; and He will enlarge our coast: and, conquerors and more than conquerors through Him who loved us, sin's usurped dominion shall be more and more impaired, and the glorious liberty wherewith Christ makes His people free be more and more enjoyed until at length "made perfect in holiness, we shall pass immediately into the full enjoying of God to all eternity."

There shall indeed be no discharge in this war so long as life shall last, for perfectness is never reached this side of the grave: but the ultimate victory is pledged beforehand to every believer: and every soldier that fights under the banner of Him who is the Captain of our salvation has the like promise given to him, which God gave to Joshua, to nerve him to effort and encourage him in every encounter. "Have not I commanded thee? Be strong and of a good courage; be not afraid, neither be thou dismayed; for the Lord thy God is with thee whithersoever thou goest."

A word or two now on the petition which remains,

"AND THAT THOU WOULDEST KEEP ME FROM EVIL, THAT IT MAY NOT GRIEVE ME."

Here may we not each one ask ourselves-How much this petition becomes us! How much it behoves us! And how confidently, yet again, we may make it a part of our prayer! It is not only in substance the petition, which our Lord has taught His disciples-"And lead us not into temptation, but deliver us from evil:" it is also our Lord's own prayer for His people, (see John xvii. 15)-"I pray not that Thou shouldest take them out of the world, but that Thou shouldest keep them from the evil."

If we know anything of ourselves or of our surroundings; anything of the inclinations within us and the influences without us, how fervently then and how frequently we will make this prayer our own-"Keep me from evil; the evil in me; the evil around me; the evil against me; the evil multiplex and manifold on every side of me. Keep me from the evil to which I am disposed; the evil from which, so insidious is it and so incessant are its attempts, that I cannot keep myself. Keep me from being drawn to it; from yielding to it; from being overcome by it. Stir me against it. Strengthen me against it. Turn me from all its forms and kinds; turn me from it unto Thee with full purpose and endeavour after new obedience! There is scarcely a prayer more germane to human need than this; for evil lurks in ambush everywhere about us; and disguised and undisguised tries hard to take and hold us in its sway.

But let us rejoice, if no prayer be more expressive of human need than this, no prayer either may be more expectant at the same time of the Divine heed. A prayer like this is a special consonance with the will of Him whose distinct declaration is, that "Evil shall not dwell with Him;" and concerning whom Paul assures in II. Thessalonians iii. 3, "But the Lord is faithful, who shall stablish you and keep you from evil."

Let us then make this petition specially and really ours. Let sin be our particular aversion. Let us hate every false way, and quit every vain thought. Let us lay aside every weight and the sin which doth most easily beset us. And let us too be sure also that shunning sin we shall at the same time avoid sorrow; and that pursuing holiness, we shall, as we overtake it, catch up upon happiness as well.

Jabez, as we saw already in this petition and in the words he appends to it, alludes evidently to the significance of his name which means 'the sorrowful,' and prays that his significance though in his name shall not be in his story.

In doing this he traces sorrow, we may safely say, to its true source and centre. It was sin which introduced it into our world at first; and sin is the baleful substance which has cast the doleful shadow of sorrow over all our history ever since. Would we be rid of sorrow then, we must get rid of sin. Peter puts the matter truly, and puts it in a nutshell when he describes "the bond of iniquity" as being also "the gall of bitterness:" and all experience is full of endorsement to the wise man's statements on the one hand, that "the way of the transgressor is hard;" and on the other, that wisdom's ways "are ways of pleasantness and all her paths are peace."

It may seem, indeed, at times and in cases as if it were otherwise. The 73rd Psalm voices a modern as well as ancient puzzle. It does seem very often still as if it where the ungodly who prospered in the world, and who had all that heart could wish-as if God's people, if marked out for any superiority at all, were marked out for extra suffering. But this is only to judge by the outward appearances: it is only a superficial review and reckoning. Take the sinner at his very best; and, did you know the whole, you would be certain to find that "even in laughter his heart is sorrowful and the end of his greatest mirth is heaviness."

Take, too, the Christian even in his worst estate; and he "can glory in tribulations; knowing that tribulation worketh patience; and patience experience; and experience hope; and hope maketh not ashamed, because the love of God is shed abroad in his heart by the Holy Ghost given unto us."

No doubt there are often troubles in a good man's life: troubles of many kinds; troubles from various causes; troubles sometimes very sore: but then, these troubles are wide in their differences from those of sinful men. They are but the pruning of the vine; but purifyings of the gold; but the chastisement of the Father who loves while He smites; and smites because He loves: and the Christian under them all has or should have such a consciousness of the love, such a confidence in it, that he can say-

Patiently received from Thee,
Evil cannot evil be:
Evil is by evil healed;
Evil is but good concealed.

He knows, that is to say, that the evils, which he endures, are evil simply in seeming; and that really goods in sequel, they only come to leave behind them, as a solid and satisfactory compensation for the very sorest of them, a great and grateful residuum of blessing. Besides, he also knows that "the sufferings of this present time are not worthy to be compared to the glory which shall be revealed in him."

Let us not be mistaken here: happiness is only to be reached and is certain to be reached by the way of holiness. Sin, on the other hand, however outwardly it may otherwise appear, is a sure forerunner of sorrow. "The wicked worketh a deceitful work; but to him that soweth righteousness shall be a sure reward." Hear Solomon when he has exhausted every expedient of irreligious experiment in search of joy. He says (see Eccles.ii.11)-"Then I looked on all the works that my hands had wrought, and on the labour that I had laboured to do: and behold, all was vanity and vexation of spirit, and there was no profit under the sun." Hear David, his father, on the other hand, even when his fortunes where at their lowest ebb- and when an exile from the tabernacle and from his throne at Jerusalem he must have keenly felt the rebellion of his son and disaffection of his people: (or perhaps he said it rather then, when Nabal churlishly refused provisions for himself and for his men)-He can sing nevertheless,

> Upon my heart bestowed by Thee,
> More gladness I have found,
> Than they, even then, when corn and wine
> Did most with them abound."

Hear Habakkuk similarly, "Although the fig tree shall not blossom, neither shall fruit be in the vines; the labour of the olive shall fail, and the fields shall yield no meat; the flock shall be cut off from the fold, and there shall be no herd in the stalls: yet will I rejoice in the Lord, I will joy in the God of my salvation." The Christian's joy is a perennial fountain springing up into everlasting life.

Its source and its supply are alike inexhaustable. Its secret and its sequel, the world can neither give nor take away. Its superiority to every earth-born joy is "as the heavens are high above the earth." It is a joy peerless and perpetual: abundant and abiding.

But we must close. Look now for a moment at the simple yet significant statement which ends the story of Jabez,

"AND GOD GRANTED HIM THAT WHICH HE REQUESTED."

Surely then we may joyfully say-here are most reassuring words for everyone of us. So we may be sure, since there is no variableness with God neither shadow of turning, it always is and will be. Whenever, wherever, by whomsoever, and as to whatsoever there is real prayer to God; then and there to everyone and in everything, God will fulfil His promise, "Ask and ye shall recieve, seek and ye shall find, knock and it shall be opened unto you:" for, note when our Saviour gives that promise duplicates it, and widens it by the supplement, "for everyone thet asketh, receiveth; and he that seeketh, findeth; and to him that knocketh it shall be opened." He asks us also, "if the fathers of our flesh being evil, knoweth how to give good gifts unto their children, how much more shall your heavenly Father give good things to them that ask Him?"

What a privilege then prayer is! and what a power! and how much more than yet we have done, we should put its power to the proof; and experience the privilege in its exercise!

Let us then in glad and grateful recognition of God's own invitation to do so-"Cast all our cares upon Him," rejoicing in the fact, though we must wonder at it too, that "He careth for us."

And while we do so, let us carry away this special lesson from Jabez here: let our first petition and our chiefest be and always be, that is, in all our supplications for ourselves; and let our every other such petition be but a detail and development of this-"Oh that Thou wouldest bless me indeed."

We are always safest and always surest of real blessing when in confiding trustfulness we leave it unreservedly to God's will and to God's wisdom, what shapes His answer to our prayers will take.

And then too let this petition principally mean with us, as really it does and must mean in its highest, truest sense-a desire to be found in, and to be conformed to the image of, His Son. Jesus Christ our Lord is God's best and greatest gift-His unspeakable gift; and above and beyond all others, far above and far beyond them-"Blessed are all they that put their trust in Him." The man who from any cause was a Jabez before, a son of sorrow, shall then when he comes to Christ, and in proportion as he cleaves to Him, become a Barnabas instead-"a son of Consolation."

Blessed are the men whose hearts are set
To find the way to Zion's gate.
God is their strength; and through the road
They lean upon their helper, God.
Cheerful they go with growing strengh
Till all shall meet in Heaven at length-
Till all before God's face appear,
And join in endless worship there.

Just note too, as one additional word in closing, that Jabez is here said to have been "more" honourable than his brethren. We may evidently infer from this, that his brothers were good and worthy too; but that Jabez, worthiest amongst the worthy, stood yet head and shoulders, spiritually highest, in estimation with men and in esteem with God. And so, may we not learn here, as a parting lesson, that while others may be eminent from other causes, and may be in some respects, in many respects, excellent and esteemed; yet above all other men it is true especially of him who prays and in whose case earnest prayer is the preparation and prelude to his every action, that he "excelleth them all;" and that he is, and always and everywhere is, pre-eminently "The man whom THE KING delighteth to honour."

Nor shall simply the mere pomp and parade of royal estate and equipage be his, and his, too, but for a day, after the fleeting fashion in which only Ahasuerus honoured Mordecai. (See Esther vi. 8,9.)

Honours far more substantial and far more durable than these shall he enjoy, and enjoy eternally. For, as his "royal apparel" he shall be clothed with "the garment of salvation," and with the "broidered work" of heavenly favours. As his kingly conveyance, he shall have the "chariot, paved with love for the daughters of Jerusalem." As the crown for his head, he shall here be "crowned with loving-kindness and tender mercies;" and he shall have hereafter "a crown of righteousness." As to his royal attendants, angels shall be his "ministering spirits:" and by and by, summoning him up higher from earth to heaven, "the King of Kings" shall invite him to His palace, saying "Come thou over with Me, and I will feed thee with Me in Jerusalem."

For hear God speaks Himself as to the way in which He honours each who trusts and serves Him- "Because he hath set his love upon Me, therefore will I deliver him: I will set him on high because he hath known My name. He shall call upon Me, and I will answer him: I will be with him in trouble: I will deliver him and honour him. With long life will I satisfy him and show him My salvation."

(See Psalm xci. 14-16.)

FRANCIS WILLMORE DIXON

Francis Willmore Dixon came to the Lord in a remarkable way. While he was on holiday at Bexhill-on-Sea with a friend, W.P.Nicholson was holding an evangelistic campaign in a tin tabernacle in the town. Francis' landlady encouraged the two young men to go and hear him. During the service God spoke to them both through the powerful preaching of God's servant. Francis came to realise his desperate need and trusted the Lord Jesus Christ as his personal Saviour.

Three days after his conversion, he was reading his Bible and came across our Lord's words, "The Spirit of the Lord is upon me because He has anointed me to preach the gospel." Francis knew from that moment God's plan for him was that he should preach the Gospel and that the Spirit was on him for this work.

In 1946 he was called to be the pastor of Lansdowne Baptist Church, Bournemouth where he continued to exercise a powerful ministry both in evangelism and bible teaching. His ministry at Keswick was just part of a convention ministry which took him all over Britain and into many parts of the world.

On Friday 18th January 1985 he left this sphere of consecrated service for more glorious service in heaven with his Lord.

This sermon on *The Prayer for True Prosperity* was preached by him on the 24th October 1967 at Lansdowne Baptist Church.

Chapter Nine

THE PRAYER FOR TRUE PROSPERITY

Perhaps the greatest privilege that God has entrusted to His children is that of the praying for other people. It is a ministry which is open to every believer and it is impossible to estimate how much can be accomplished by it-look up James 5:17. When we realise how much blessing can be brought unto the lives of others by our prayers for them we at once see how much we deprive them of it if we fail to pray for them-look up 1 Samuel 12:23. It is also important to notice that there is great blessing for ourselves when we pray for others-look up Job 42:10. In this study, however, we are not to think so much about praying for other people but about praying for ourselves. In Chronicles 4: 9-10, we read of Jabez who was a man of prayer. There is no doubt at all that he prayed for others, but the particular emphasis that is made in these two verses is that he prayed for himself. It is not selfish to pray for ourselves, for it is only as we our blessed that we can be a blessing to others. It was when Jabez prayed for true prosperity, and the Lord answered that prayer, that he could be made of inestimable blessing to other people. A careful study of the prayer of Jabez shows us that it contained four characteristics.

(1) *Jabez prayed Intelligently.* We are told that he "called on the God of Israel"-that is to say, the Covenant God, the true and living God. It evident that Jabez had been instructed in the school of prayer, and therefore his prayer was informed and intelligent. Very much prayer is unintelligent and is therefore unprofitable, and for an example of this look up Luke 18: 11-12. The fundamental condition of prayer is that we must know God as our loving Heavenly Father-look up Matthew 6 and compare verses 6 and 9.

(2) *Jabez prayed Earnestly.* Notice the intensity of his prayer. This was borne in upon him as he cried out to the Lord. He did not simply say "Lord, bless me!", but "Oh that Thou wouldest bless me indeed...!" We cannot fail to detect the reality, indeed, the agony and the passion that are present in this earnest cry to God. This must surely challenge us, for often we pray passionless, half-hearted prayers, and is it any wonder, therefore, that such prayers do not reach the Throne of Heavenly grace?-look up Genesis 32:26. and compare Luke 11: 5-10 and Luke 18: 1-8.

(3) *Jabez prayed Definitely.* When Jabez prayed he knew what he wanted and he asked for what he wanted: there was nothing haphazard about his praying. His prayer was preceded by careful thought and meditation, and when he came to the moment of presenting his petition he was able to make his request in clear defined terms. How important it is to be definite when we pray!-look up 1 Samuel 1: 10-11.

(4) *Jabez prayed Effectually.* When Jabez prayed, "God granted him that which he requested". There is tremendous encouragement in these words, for the God of Jabez is our God, and just as God answered this man's prayer so He has pledged His word to do the same for us-look up and compare Jeremiah 33: 3; Mark 11: 24; John 15:7 and James 4:2.

These then are the four characteristics of this amazing prayer that Jabez offered for himself: Jabez prayed intelligently, earnestly, definitely and effectually, for his prayer was wonderfully answered. Now notice from this prayer of Jabez how to pray that God will give you true prosperity. In verse 10 we are told that Jabez prayed for four things. Thy are clearly mentioned, and we cannot do better than follow this man's example and pray as he prayed:-

(1) *We should pray for Grace.* Jabez prayed, "Oh that Thou wouldest bless me indeed...!" What did he mean by this request? Every believer is already wonderfully blessed-look up Ephesians 1:3; but sure Jabez was praying for Divine enabling without which he could never be the man God wanted him to be-see what Paul said in 1 Corinthians 15:10. If we would be what God wants us to be it can only be by His grace: therefore let us pray for grace, and there is plenty of grace available- look up 2 Corinthians 9:8! In 1 Chronicles 4:9 there is a hint concerning a possible reason why Jabez needed special grace, for his name means 'sorrowful'. Perhaps there was some secret tragedy concerning his birth - but whatever it was he needed grace and he prayed for grace, and of course he recieved the grace he needed, just as we will receive the grace we need-look up 2 Corinthians 12:9.

(2) *We should pray for Growth.* How beautiful it is to hear Jabez saying to the Lord, "Oh, that Thou wouldest....enlarge my coast!"- compare 2 Peter 3:18. Many Christians are content to remain in a state of babyhood-look up 1 Corinthians 3: 1-2. We need to pray that the Lord will enlarge our coast, increase our capacity, deepen our faith, inflame our love, give us more opportunities, make us more usable and conform us more to the image of His Son-look up Romans 8:29. It is a very costly thing to ask the Lord to enlarge your coast undoubtedly it will mean testing, for it is by testing that we grow. Without testing we remain dwarfs, we remain flabby and ineffective, but if the Lord is to make us strong for Him we must be tested-look up 1 Peter 1:7.

(3) *We should pray for guidance.* Jabez prayed.... "that Thine hand might be with me." The hand of God is an expression that denotes the power of the living God in action-look up Ezra 7:9, and

compare Psalm 139:5. God wants us to live a guided life-look up Psalm 37:23. He has made provision for our lives to be "ordered", as Whittier expressed it so beautifully:-

"Drop Thy still dews of quietness.
Till all our strivings cease;
Take from our souls the strain and stress;
And let our ordered lives confess
The beauty of Thy peace."

How grand and how glorious a thing it is when the striving, the strain and the stress are taken out of our lives and when, because the hand of the Lord is with us and upon us, we are enabled to live ordered lives and experience the beauty of His peace!

(4) *We should pray for Godliness.* Jabez prayed, "....that Thou wouldest keep me from evil, that it may not grieve me", or, "that it might not spoil my life." What a prayer to pray! It reminds us of 2 Timothy 4:18. and thank God, the Lord is able to deliver us from evil and enable us to live a life that is glorifying to Him, a life that is pure, holy and Christ-like!

In verse 9, Jabez is described as God's "honourable" man. Why is this? What is the secret of becoming one of God's honourable ones? The secret is-prayer, much prayer and more prayer-look up 1 Thessalonians 5:17.

ALEXANDER RALEIGH D.D.

A lexander Raleigh D.D. was born on 3rd January 1817 in Kirkcudbright, Scotland. After a village school education he worked for a short time in Liverpool before deciding to study theology at Blackburn College.

He was ordained as pastor of the Independent Chapel at Greenock, Scotland in 1844 but due to ill health he was compelled to resign in 1848.

From 1850 to 1855 he lived at Rotherham, England but returned to Scotland and settled in Glasgow until 1859, when he moved to London, remaining there until his death on the 19th April 1880.

He was eminently a spiritually minded man and his works *Quiet Resting-places and Other Sermons; The Story of Jonah the Prophet, The Little Sanctuary, and Other Meditations; The Book of Esther* and *Thoughts for the Weary and the Sorrowful* have been a great blessing to many.

This sermon on the Prayer of Jabez was taken from *The Way to the City and Other Sermons*.

Chapter Ten

BLESSING AND ENLARGEMENT

⌒

And Jabez was more honourable than his brethren: and his mother
called his name Jabez saying, because I bare him with sorrow!
And Jabez called on the God of Israel saying, Oh that Thou
wouldest bless me indeed, and enlarge my coast, and that Thine
hand might be with me, and that Thou wouldest keep me from evil,
that it may not grieve me! And God granted him that which he
requested.- CHRON.iv. 9,10.

⌒

This little history of Jabez, in two verses, is full of interest and beauty.
We come upon it as it were suddenly, and with a kind of surprise, as
one who travelling through a rocky mountainous country, comes all
at once upon some little green dell, watered with streams, and filled
with beauty.

This narrative of the Chronicles, consisting as it does of a series
of names, although valuable and necessary, may be called the rocky
or desert part of holy Scripture; and in traversing this desert, as we
go by historic line from one part to another of the great realm of
divine truth, lo! we are stayed when we reach this point, and affected
with involuntary admiration. The narrative softens and glows with

a living beauty. This man Jabez stands out from the long ranks, "more honourable than his brethren." He is like Saul among the people by his moral elevation. He is the very opposite of his name-"Jabez," "sorrowful." He is a bright, strong, joyful man, spreading strength and joy to others, and his memorial in Israel is blessed.

"His mother called him Jabez, because she bare him with sorrow." Whether it was the usual sorrow of child birth intensified in her case into some great danger, or whether she had some other sorrow resting heavily on her at the time, or indeed what was precisely the cause of her melancholy dejection, and of the name given to her child as a sad and salutary reminiscence of it, we cannot tell. But, mothers, you see the beautiful fact that the child comes to you in great sorrow, or in a dark and sorrowful time, and whom you name Jabez or Benoni in your sadness, may get the benefit of your sufferings and of your prayers, carry all that benefit up into his life, become to his father a Benjamin, a man of his right hand, and to you, his mother, a protector and joy.

In what Jabez was "more honourable," we are not told.

It might be in *courage*, for these were struggling, fighting times, when courage was greatly needed; when courage was, in fact, a form of piety and obedience. If he had been signalisied chiefly by modesty, meekness, patience, retirement, he never would have had his "coast enlarged." He prayed for that, and no doubt he also fought for that. Cannanites and Philistines were not to be propitiated and endured; they were to be overcome and expelled. There are certain spiritual Cannanities always, while the Church is militant, who are to be met, not with the soft airs of charity, with proposals for truce or concilation, but with sword and spear and battle-axe, until they are destroyed.

Or it might be for *learning* that Jabez was more honourable than his brethren. In Chron. ii. 55, there is a city mentioned called Jabez, so named, many think, from the famous man of that name, where the families of the scribes dwelt-the men who, as public notaries wrote and signed legal instruments, or who as ecclesiastical officers, wrote and expounded the law, and taught the people. There may have been a revival of learning in the person of this man. To promote learning is an honourable thing, and to spread knowledge of any kind, but especially of the highest kind, in any way-by books, if there is anything in them, by schools, by colleges, by teaching or preaching-is good; and that man distinguishes himself, makes himself "honourable," who in any way spreads light among his fellowmen.

In any case it is certain that Jabez was more honourable *for his piety.* And perhaps, after all, this is the chief thing intended, for in close connection, we have the record of his prayer.

This prayer was probably composed and offered when he was undertaking some great enterprise, which was attended with much peril. Probably, also, it became a characteristic and continuous prayer of his life. It was the liturgy of his heart. It was his daily service. He was always praying this prayer. Let us look at the elements of it, and let us apply them, as far as we can, to our own engagements, to our own daily life, to our own soul-state.

ONE

Jabez *called on the God of Israel.* He declared himself a religious man; a worshipper of Jehovah, the true God. He did this publicly and conspicuously, on some one occasion, probably for the first time, before his people, in the presence of his soldiers perhaps, when going forth to the battle; proclaiming, in presence of them all, his helplessness and his dependence on God. But he did it always. "He called on the God of Israel." It was the habit of his life; it was the action of each separate day; he was known by *this*; this lay at the foundation of his courage, his goodness, his success.

Need I say that this still lies at the foundation of individual prosperity and goodness of the highest kind? Personal religion-calling upon God. Without this there cannot be any beginning of progress that will avail in the end. A man living without this is not truely living at all. A man whose soul never "calls," never cries, never looks, never waits upon God, is not living to the end for which a man should live. He is not truly a man. He is guilty of the awful sin of making himself less than himself. He is darkening his own being, repressing its powers, limiting its exertions, stifling its voices! For it is true as truth can be, that the glory of a man is the knowledge and love and service of God.

What is it that raises a man above the brutes, not merely in degree, but in very nature, leaving between them a great space which cannot be bridged? Not the possession, by man, of natural reason simply, for animals reason in there own way. When we deny them the possession of reason, and call there wisest actions the results of instinct, we simply flee from a difficulty under cover of a name. There is an immense difference in degree, but it would be hard to make out a clear difference in kind, between the reason of the animal and that of the man. When you come into the moral region the difference is more apparent and more wide, although, even there, the animal seems to have in its nature some shadowings of the human conscience, seems to perform some actions which we can hardly call less than good. It would be hard to deny some moral merit to the dog which watched by the dead body of its master for three long months, on the solitary snowy hights of the Helvellyn, "To drive the hill-fox and the raven away."

But when you come up into the sphere of religion, into the world of worship, you find only man. He alone of all the creatures is so endowed that he stands consciously before the face of the personal God, the Maker, the Ruler of all. He only can worship and adore. He only can reverence, and love, and serve an unseen Being. He only can discover his soul's parentage, and obey the Father of spirits. But if he neglects all this; if he never does call upon the God of Israel; if he goes about the world with a dumb soul, with a blind religious faculty within him, with a yearning that never has expression, with fears he dares not tell, is he not making himself less than himself? Is he not doing violence to his very manhood? And if a man is thus wrong in the great relation, and untrue to all that is best in himself, what boots it what he says, what he seems, what he gets, what he does? He can only build on the sand. He can only write on the air. He can only plough the ocean. He can only sow on rocks and by the beaten waysides. The flowers of the garden of his life might be gay, but they are withering. The pictures that hang on the walls of his imagination may be bright, but every colour is already stained. O lonely man! I see him in a while companionless and sad-a wreck-a misery to himself-a living loss, which, but for God's mercy, may prove eternal.

Call upon the God of Israel! you whom this matter concerns. "Seek ye the Lord, while He may be found; call ye upon Him while He is near." He is saying to you now, "Seek ye My face." He has said that many a time already, and in many a way. He has said it by the inward feeling of your vast need, and by the sense of sin which has sometimes struck you like an arrow, and for a moment pained you at the heart! and by the swell of a great desire, like the lifting of the tide sometimes in your bosom! And by the changes and providences of your life, and by the uncertainties of the future, and by swift-coming death, and by solemn judgement beyond, and by the voice of Christ, and by the striving of the Spirit, and by all the rich mercies of our God. "What meanest thou, O sleeper? arise, and call upon thy God!"

TWO

Calling, what does Jabez say? "Oh that Thou wouldest bless me indeed!" So far it might be said that this prayer is not very definite. But, perhaps, it is all the better, as expressive of many a condition of life, and especially the state of one who is just *beginning* to pray. A man awaking out of sleep has at first only confused ideas, a dim sight of things, only part possession of himself. So one awaking to a sense of God, and of himself as God's creature and child, is sometimes confused, perplexed, anxious-hardly knows what to think, what to ask for-and is glad, at length, to throw his soul, as it were, into a sigh, to send up such a general ejaculation as this, that shall be sure to have all petitions in one. "Oh that Thou wouldest bless me indeed!" I know not what to say before Thee, how to tell my needs, how to confess my sin, how to mourn over my ingratitude, how to take returning steps. I have been far away, and I am stumbling homewards now; I have been dead, but I seem to be now coming alive again; I was lost, but surely this is my finding. "Oh that Thou wouldest bless me indeed!"

The prayer is earnest, it glows along every syllable. It has in it the tension and pressure made by a great desire. Heaven and earth tell, and hell too, that unless a man is earnest he cannot enter into life.

The prayer is not only earnest. It is full of a particular kind of thirst or desire, the desire for God. It goes right up to Him, without circumlocution, without deflection. It recognises His supremacy, His all sufficiency, His power to bless! There is no tone of doubt in it, in this regard, "Oh that thou wouldest." Thou canst if Thou wilt. The sufficiency of power is generally seen before the sufficiency of the love.

It is a thorough prayer, a through and through prayer. "Oh that Thou wouldest bless me indeed!" I do not want a partial blessing, touching only a part of my nature, supplying only a part of my need. I do not want a transient blessing, that shall go up from from my heart like the dew of the morning, leaving me dry, and dusty, and barren again. I want a blessing that shall flow along the channel of my life. So much might any man find in the prayer, and express it by his first returnings and approaches to God, short, and simple, and general as it is. An expression like this really meets a need-a sorely felt need-of many souls. In conscious sin and guilt, in weakness, confusion, and fear, a man knows not what to say. Then, bethinking him that God is greater than the heart, and knoweth all things, and will therefore give interpretation to all the misery, all the penitence, all the longing, and all the love; that He will hear the grownings that cannot be uttered; that He will take dim thoughts for words, and hear the souls inmost desires, although so poorly told; the man is content, and with a cry of relief, as well as earnestness, he says, "Oh that thou wouldest bless me indeed!"

If this was to Jabez a kind of liturgy, as we have supposed-a little daily service-a heart-book of common prayer-then it ought to be suitable to a man long after the first awaking and returning time.

It is not so? Are we not glad sometimes, through weariness, when we have not strengh to make prolonged and specific prayer; and sometimes, through perplexity and trouble, when we know not what to ask for; and sometimes, in mood of sadness and seriousness, or of spiritual ambition, when we only have the desire, and know not whence it is, nor by what grace of God it may be met and satisfied; are we not glad, I say, to throw all into something like this brief supplication, and say, "Oh that Thou wouldest bless me indeed"? In the morning, when you are going forth to your labour, and somehow don't feel yourself sufficiently shielded and supplied, take the broad buckler of this prayer of Jabez, and all divine protection will be over you.

THREE

But there is something more definite immediatley, "Oh that Thou wouldest bless me,"... "and *enlarge my coast.*" He prays for more territory to his people and himself-more power-more wealth. These are what we should call earthly and temporal blessings. But he did not regard them in that light chiefly. The best men of the Old Testament did not distinguish between temporal and spiritual, as we do. Nor do I think that by our principle of distinguishing the one from the other sharply, we transcend these fathers of our faith-we rather fall below them, in this. Their view of things was simpler, and essentially more spiritual, that the view which some take, i.e. than this world, with its affairs and its possessions, is comparatively unclean and unprofitable.

Jacob made a covenant, what we should call quite *a bargain*, about temporal things with God-bread to eat, and raiment to put on, and health and preservation through coming years, and a safe and prosperous return to his own land-and this he did immediately after what we may call his conversion, after one of the most wonderful scenes of his life, after he had dreamed that glorious dream, and trodden the awful house of God, and stood at the bright gate of heaven.

Hannah came up to the very altar of God, grieved and weeping, to ask for a little child from God; and the asking was so direct and earnest and intense about this thing, that when he came she could call him nothing but Samuel, "asked for." And Jabez has no sooner called upon God for blessing than he asks for increase of land-the "enlargement of his coast," as a part of this very blessing: I think it is beautiful. Life was a spiritual unity to these men. They had no dividing lines, and it would be better for us if we had none, if life were all one piece, all one enterprise, all one great service to God.

As soon as a man stands consciously and willingly under and in the great blessing of God, one of the most appropriate desires he can have, is just this desire of enlargement. "Enlarge my coast." When a man's sins are pardoned, and his life rectified, when his motive is pure, and his purpose right, when his soul is nourished with the blessing of God, one cannot but think the more of that man the better. Let him be enlarged! For a recompense of the same, let him be enlarged! Give him room! Give him means! Give him trust and honour! If he is a plant of the Lord's right hand planting, let him grow!

"Heaven send him happy dew,
Earth lend him sap anew
Gaily to burgeon, and broadly to grow!"

Do you say there is danger in growing? so there is in not growing. Danger in getting? so there is in not getting; so there is in losing. Do you say that an expanding life multiplies dangers? No doubt, but it also multiplies the grace, if it be expansion on the right principle.

"Moored in the rifted rock,
Proof to the tempest's shock,
Firmer he roots him the ruder it blow."

When a worldly penurious man makes money, that is not enlargement in the grand sense at all. He is making chains to hold captive, and in a while they will be on his own limbs. He is building a prison, and himself will be the prisoner. An old man, in his last illness, was recieved at one of the metropolitan hospitals. He was without relation or friends-a lonely old man, and to all appearances without resources. But a bag of money was found round his neck. He wore it next his heart, and clung to it with the utmost tenacity; the nurses could not remove it. He was sinking fast, and at length the final hour arrived. When death had apparently claimed him, a nurse gently unfastened the string and removed the bag. At the same moment the old man opened his eyes, and felt instinctively for his treasure which was no longer in its place. He uttered the word "Gone!" and died. The money amounted to £174, the accumulation no doubt, of many years. But was that man "enlarged" as the process went on? He was narrowed and crippled. Every golden piece he added to that bag was adding to the weight he carried, in more sense than one, until it became a millstone about his neck, and drowned him in death.

And who can doubt that many a one is restricted and burdened and filled with restless cares, and selfish cravings, by all the outward enlargement that comes to him? His coast, in the spiritual sense is not "enlarged" but limited and drawn in, until at length the soul has hardly breathing-room; and from many a death-bed there goes up at last that old man's sigh, "Gone!" money "gone;" houses "gone;" broad acres "gone;" name and fame "gone." All that has been striven for through a lifetime "gone!" Ah! poor fatal enlargement that ends in such collapse! The true enlargement is such that a catastrophe like this is quiet impossible. The man with soul enlarged, does he ever sigh, in death or in life, "Gone"? No. "Going with me, wherever I go, all that is most valued, all that is best, I have chosen the good part that shall not be taken away."

This is it in brief. If only we are careful to seek and find the blessing of the Lord indeed, and if we shape and rule our life so that we may keep that blessing still, and have it growing in all our growth, and shining in all our pleasure and beauty, and working in all our industry, and running on through all our days, then we may seek enlargement without fear. We ought to seek it. A man's life is not worth much if it ceases to be capable of enlargement.

Why should such a man not seek money in due subordination to other things? Because "the love of money is the root of all evil"? True. But the use of it is the channel of all good. Why should he not seek social influence? Because "the friendship of the world is enmity with God"? True; but he is the salt and the light of that very world. Why should he not seek knowledge and culture, sensibility, all that refines and makes men noble? Because "in much wisdom is much grief, and he that increaseth knowledge increaseth sorrow"? True;

but in much folly and ignorance is found much more grief, and out of sorrow comes a larger joy. No; the thing we have to fear is not the enlargement in itself, but possible harm and danger to us in the process-perversion, corruption,-the coming in of the hurtful elements.

Jabez seems to have feared this, and he prays against it.

FOUR

The summing up of the prayer. "And that Thine hand might be with me, and that Thou wouldest keep me from evil, that it may not grieve me." Wherever I am be Thou with me. Whatsoever I do, be Thou the strengh of it; keep me from evil-the evil that arises from within-from perversion of principle, from the corruption of motive, from defective aims, from selfishness, cruelty, uncharitableness, from the evil heart of unbelief. Keep me from the evil that is sure to come surging upon me from without. The sword of the Canaanite. The tongue of the slanderer. The terror and the pleasure and the guile of an evil world; keep me from them all; still on and on, to the very end!

So let us seek preservation from evil, inward and outward, by watchfulness, by prayer, by dependence on God, and we need never fear enlargement. Let it go on without limit and without fear, if it goes on thus, banked in on either hand by divine blessing and by divine care.

No harm came to Jabez. God granted him his prayer. He overcame his enemies. He enlarged his coast. Evil did not grieve him, because he was kept from it. God's hand was with him. The God of Israel blessed him indeed. He chanted this life-liturgy, he sang this daily psalm, he prayed this prayer, in all the places and in all weathers, and "God granted him that which he requested." He grew in strengh like an oak; in beauty like a flower. He stood out a pillar-man, a mountain-man, even in his own generation. He stands conspicuous still. "More honourable than his brethren;" who knows anything about them? When will his glory fade? "Happy Jabez! for that thou hast lived already a thousand lives. Thou hast made thy life a river that shall roll on for the refreshing of the ages!" And there is no man nor woman-how young, how weak, how poor soever-who may not be a Jabez in his or her own place and way.

But observe; the condition of conditions is this-that you seek-yes, until you find-divine blessing. Put that first in your life-a blessing that shall purge away your sins through the great Sacrifice; that shall regenerate heart and soul, and strength and mind; a blessing that shall pass through you like fire to consume all that is evil, and then rest on your heart like dew, to nourish all that is good; which will go with you as a living presence, shedding light, and power, and comfort as you need them; which, in fact, will not leave you until you spring from the shadows and limitations of mortality into the largeness and clearness of immortal life.

O seek, and you shall find! ask, and it shall be given unto you! If Jabez found in that long ago time, how shall not you? now that God has been manifested in the flesh, now that Christ has come, now that He has died, yea, rather, has risen again; now that He gives to all that are athirst "of the water of life freely"?

**Other titles written / compiled by
Stanley Barnes include:**

All For Jesus – The Life of W. P. Nicholson

Goodbye God - Stirring Messages by W. P. Nicholson

An Inspirational Treasury of D. L. Moody

An Inspirational Treasury of Samuel Rutherford

God Makes A Path – A Devotional from the Writings of
R. M. McCheyne

Sermons on John 3:16

Sermons on Isaiah 63

Sermons on Acts 16

Visit our web site for updates
www.ambassador-productions.com